Performance-Based
Assessment
FOR 21ST-CENTURY SKILLS

Performance-Based Assessment

FOR 21ST-CENTURY SKILLS

- Provides real-world examples -
- Breaks down the process into easy steps -
- Contains ready-to-use reproducibles -

TODD STANLEY

PRUFROCK PRESS INC.

WACO, TEXAS

Library of Congress Cataloging-in-Publication Data

Stanley, Todd.
  Performance-based assessment for 21st-century skills / by Todd Stanley.
    pages cm
  Includes bibliographical references.
  ISBN 978-1-61821-273-3 (pbk.)
  1. Educational tests and measurements--United States. 2. Students--Rating of--United States. I. Title.
  LB3051.S865 2014
  371.26--dc23
                        2014017053

Edited by Rachel Taliaferro

Cover design by Raquel Trevino and layout design by Allegra Denbo

ISBN-13: 978-1-61821-273-3

Printed in the United States of America.

At the time of this book's publication, all facts and figures cited are the most current available. All telephone numbers, addresses, and website URLs are accurate and active. All publications, organizations, websites, and other resources exist as described in the book, and all have been verified. The author and Prufrock Press Inc. make no warranty or guarantee concerning the information and materials given out by organizations or content found at websites, and we are not responsible for any changes that occur after this book's publication. If you find an error, please contact Prufrock Press Inc.

Prufrock Press Inc.
P.O. Box 8813
Waco, TX 76714-8813
Phone: (800) 998-2208
Fax: (800) 240-0333
http://www.prufrock.com

Table of Contents

What Is Performance-Based Assessment?

Before you begin to figure out just exactly how you are going to use performance-based assessment (PBA) in your classroom, it is important to have a good understanding of the subject matter. Math teachers need to understand equations in order to teach them to students, and language arts instructors need to have a good grasp of grammar if they expect their students to follow suit. If you want to use PBA in your classroom and make it effective, it is important you understand what it is and what you can do with it. Like most things in education, there can be multiple interpretations of a concept. Let us start with a simple definition and work our way to a more complex one.

According to the Project Appleseed (2010) website, the Office of Technology Assessment of the U.S. Congress describes performance assessments as: " . . . testing that requires a student to create an answer or a product that demonstrates his or her knowledge or skills" (para. 2). That is a pretty simple and broad definition. A clever gifted student could probably make a compelling argument that filling in bubbles on a multiple-choice test is "creating an answer," but in the spirit of the definition, objective assessments such as multiple-choice tests do not qualify as performance-based assessments. However, writing an essay does qualify as creating—the student must create his answer, deciding how to state the information he wants to include to construct his thesis. Again, our illustrious gifted student might make an argument that this is not a performance. He might say that a performance should be a display of skills, like acting out a play or playing a musical instrument. Writing an essay *is* a display of skills, however—one that demonstrates what the student knows. That much is evident from this more complex definition of performance-based assessment from Project Appleseed (2010):

> Performance assessment requires students to demonstrate knowledge and skills, including the process by which they solve problems. Performance assessments measure skills such as the ability to integrate knowledge across disciplines, contribute to the work of a group, and develop a plan of action when confronted with a new situation. (para. 1)

The key word in this definition is *process*. Performance-based assessment is a process. Student learning is not displayed only in the summative assessments traditional classes give at the end of a unit. What students learn is on display throughout the process of working on an activity. Sometimes this is a concrete product, such as a physical object that students build, or an intangible product, such as a fact they display through an essay. Other times the performance is less concrete, when a student is asked to think creatively or to overcome a problem. Getting the right answer is not necessarily the end-all, be-all goal. How students arrive at an answer can be just as, if not more, important than the answer itself.

Given this definition, it probably sounds as if just about anything could be considered a performance-based assessment. However, there are certain guidelines PBAs generally follow. For instance, the National Science Foundation's (2003; Stevenson, 2001) science and engineering indicators suggest performance-based assessments usually:

- allow students to create their own response rather than to choose between several already created answers,
- are criterion-referenced, or provide a standard according to which a student's work is evaluated rather than in comparison with other students,
- concentrate on the problem-solving process rather than on just obtaining the correct answer, and
- require that trained teachers or others carefully evaluate the assessments and provide consistency across scorers (Stevenson, 2001, para. 4).

We will explore these guidelines in much more depth later in the book.

These different definitions of and parameters for PBA are all very well and good, but what does the actual process look like? If I walked into a class in which a teacher was using performance-based assessment, what would I see? Below are some examples according to Project Appleseed (2010):

- group projects enabling a number of students to work together on a complex problem that requires planning, research, internal discussion, and group presentation;
- essays assessing students' understanding of a subject through a written description, analysis, explanation, or summary;
- experiments testing how well students understand scientific concepts and can carry out scientific processes;
- demonstrations giving students opportunities to show their mastery of subject-area content and procedures; or
- portfolios allowing students to provide a broad portrait of their performance through files that contain collections of students' work assembled over time (para. 3).

Now that you have a basic understanding of what performance-based assessment is and what it might look like, it is time to explain this book's three goals: (1) to convince you why performance-based assessment should be used over other methods of teaching, (2) to show how it can be used in the classroom for effective student understanding, and (3) to show where it can take you as a teacher in your professional development.

I hope this introduction gives you a basic understanding of what performance-based assessment is. The first chapter of this book will make a compelling case for why a teacher should use performance-based assessment and the 21st-century skills it builds in students. Chapter 2 will discuss the advantages of using PBA in the classroom, including what it will allow a teacher to do with students that more traditional methods will not and why these are beneficial to teaching and learning. Chapter 3 will explore in more depth various examples of PBA and what skills each one will provide for students. Chapter 4 will explain how to teach students the ways they can use PBA to its fullest extent. Because students are sometimes used to a more traditional setting, they must be trained how to use PBA. One of the most pressing questions when using PBA is how one should evaluate it. This is one of the trickiest aspects of PBA and one that must be deliberate in its set-up and execution. Chapter 5 will walk you through the steps of how to make this happen. Chapter 6 will take the concept of authentic assessment, a valuable part of any PBA classroom, and show you how to achieve it. The more authentic the assessment, the more enduring the learning is going to be. The book will conclude with words of advice on how to make the PBA process work for you and how to get the most from it in your classroom. There are three appendices. The first includes reproducibles that can be used to shape your own classroom using performance-based assessment. The second appendix contains a sample lesson plan for a mock trial in an elementary classroom. The third appendix includes lessons from some major content areas and different grade levels so that you have an idea of what PBA looks like and what can be done with it.

One of the sage pieces of advice given to writers is to show the story rather than tell it. Instead of saying a character is scared, a good author will describe how the hairs on the back of the character's neck tingled with dread or how the air in her lungs built up to the point that she felt they were going to burst. This shows the reader the fear instead of simply stating it. The description is memorable and enduring. More traditional methods of assessment, such as multiple-choice tests, allow students to *tell* you what they know, but they do not *show* you how the students arrived at the answer, to what level of depth they understand it, or how they can take the information and make something new from it. In the real world, this is what you spend most of your life doing: showing, not telling. You want to get your students ready to be part of that 21st-century world.

CHAPTER 1

A Case for Performance-Based Assessment

It seems there is an objective multiple-choice test for everything. If you want to get into college, you have to take the SAT or ACT, often both. If you want to be a doctor or lawyer, you have to pass the MCAT or pass the bar exam. Even if you want to drive, you must first take a pencil-to-paper test in which you essentially determine which of four letters is more attractive than the others. The interesting aspect about all of these is that in order to show success in the field in which you take a test to get into, it always comes down to performance. You can score very high on the SAT or ACT, but in college you have to show up to classes and perform in order to succeed. As a doctor or lawyer, you may pass the MCAT or the bar, but the true merit of a successful doctor or lawyer is how well she performs in the field. Even passing the writing portion of your driver's test does not necessarily correlate with how well you will perform once you get in the car and have to maneuver the vehicle on the road. With this logic, would we not be better off having people take tests that evaluate the performance rather than a multiple-choice assessment that evaluates memorization? Would this not be a better indicator of the success a person might have once he or she actually gets in the field and has to perform in the real world?

School systems spend nearly the entire year evaluating the performance of students. How well do they participate in class? How often do they get their homework completed? Do they show a deep understanding of the material and concepts being taught? And yet at the end of the year, we have it all boil down to an objective multiple-choice test that the state has dictated must be given to all students. Since the

No Child Left Behind Act came out in 2001, we have been pushing students to tell us what they have learned on pencil-to-paper tests with a lot of accountability tied to the results. School districts are evaluated based on these scores, principals are held accountable when their schools do not perform well, and teachers feel the pressure for students to do well. Because of this, we have developed strategies for students to do better on these types of tests. One of those strategies involves modeling all assessments in the classroom so that students are familiar with both the format and the way the content is delivered. As a result, students are getting really good at filling in little bubbles. The problem is that they are losing those valuable performance-based abilities, many of which are 21st-century skills.

The powers that be in education are starting to realize the value in performance-based assessment. That is why a new state testing system, the PARCC (Partnership for Assessment of Readiness for College and Careers), will incorporate a performance aspect to it. Unlike the state tests of the past, which focus only on multiple-choice questions with some written responses, this test will be broken down into two parts. There will be the traditional end-of-year assessment in which students demonstrate their reading comprehension and mathematical problem-solving skills. The second part will be a performance assessment aspect that will look at students' ability to analyze and understand how a problem is solved. There are 20 states already planning on using the PARCC Assessment with more sure to follow.

In addition, many states are employing the Common Core State Standards (CCSS). These are learning objectives that many states are using to add rigor in the classroom and ensure we are producing 21st-century students who are ready to use these skills in a global work force. Many of the standards have the term "real world" in them just to make sure students get the point of how important being able to apply these skills in the real world is. Many of these CCSS are also written in a way that lends them to performance-based assessment. Take these examples of Common Core State Standards (National Governors Association Center for Best Practices & Council of Chief State School Officers, 2010a; 2010b):

> CCSS ELA.Literacy.W.6.7: Conduct short research projects to answer a question, drawing on several sources and refocusing the inquiry when appropriate.

> CCSS Math.Content.2.MD.D.10: Draw a picture graph and a bar graph to represent a data set with up to four categories. Solve simple put-together, take-apart, and compare problems using information presented in the bar graph.

How could a student conduct a short research project without producing a performance-based assessment, whether it is via a research paper or a presentation? Drawing picture and bar graphs are examples of PBAs in that students actually have to create something. The direction of education naturally takes us toward performance-based assessment. Wouldn't you rather be on the rising tide of this movement rather than on the end of the crashing wave?

The reason for these changes is the realization that objective testing is not necessarily causing our students to have enduring understanding. Asian schools consistently score well on international academic tests and match this assessment practice by placing a heavy emphasis on rote memorization. The problem with this is that these very same students who score so well retain the information for the least amount of time, meaning they cannot apply what they have supposedly learned (Robbins, 2006). Is our goal as educators for students to know information just long enough to score well on the test, or is the goal for students to learn the content for life? If you think our goal is to provide an enduring understanding, PBA is the method that will best produce this:

> An alternative method of evaluating students is "performance assessment," which appraises students on items such as portfolios, projects, and writing samples. Students will be more prone to "deep approach" learning rather than superficial, temporary memorization of facts, and teachers will have the chance to spend semesters actually teaching rather than reviewing for an exam. (Robbins, 2006, p. 391)

What we should be teaching our students are life-long skills they can use when needed. We could view this building of skills as creating a Swiss Army knife. Swiss Army knives have several different tools that can be utilized depending on the situation. If you need to unscrew something, pull out the screwdriver blade. If you need to open a bottle of pop, flip out the bottle opener. If you have to cut out a coupon, deploy the little pair of scissors. Even if you have a piece of corn stuck in your teeth, you can use the little toothpick attachment. You do not pull out the single large blade to try to accomplish all of these tasks because you would end up severely limited in what you could do and how well it could be done (and you would probably hurt yourself). Similarly in education, rather than teaching students one way to learn, or equipping them with only the one blade, we should be teaching them various ways to learn so that they can use the appropriate tool for the appropriate task. Performance-based assessment gives students these tools to develop their Swiss Army knives. The question is: What tools should students have in their Swiss Army knives?

The most compelling case for PBA is that it utilizes real-world skills—also known as 21st-century skills—that are valuable no matter what a student envisions her future to be. These are the skills students should be developing as their Swiss Army knives. Think of the ancient Confucian proverb: "If you give a person a fish, he eats for one day. If you teach that person to fish, he can eat for the rest of his life." In other words, if you simply give students the answers, they only know the answers and are very limited in their education. If you teach them how to *learn*, they can find the answers themselves and the sky is the limit. As a caveat to this proverb, though, you might have to teach students a few different ways to fish. In other words, if students learn only one way to fish, they may catch only one type of fish. If the stock for that fish runs out, or the students are just getting tired of having the same kind of fish over and over, or if it is just not the students' strength to fish in that way, it is good to have multiple ways to accomplish the task. The students can choose the method that best plays to their strengths. This is why teaching students multiple methods of PBA is very valuable. If you focus on a single method, you limit learning. You want your students' Swiss Army knives to have multiple blades for multiple situations.

In the book, *21st-Century Skills: Learning for Life in Our Times* by Bernie Trilling and Charles Fadel (2012), the authors mention among valuable 21st-century skills eight specific skills that PBA can teach very effectively:

- public speaking,
- problem solving,
- collaboration,
- critical thinking,
- information literacy,
- creativity,
- adaptability, and
- self-direction (p. viii).

Let us take a closer look at each of these, what the skill involves, how performance-based assessment can successfully teach it, and why it will be important to your students.

PUBLIC SPEAKING

Public speaking is an invaluable skill for any person to have. One of the major reasons for this is that not everyone is able to do it. If you are someone who can speak in public and do it well, you have an advantage over others. Many people have a fear of speaking in public. The National Institute of Mental Health indicated that 74% of Americans suffer from a fear of public speaking (Statistic Brain, 2013). That is three out of every four people. This fear of public speaking, known as *glossophobia*, is something that can be overcome, especially if you start the process before it becomes a deep-rooted fear. Experience tends to be the best coping mechanism. The more experience someone has at something, the less likely she is going to panic. An extreme example of this would be how some police departments train their officers to deal with a dog attack. They put their officers in a padded suit and then turn an attack dog loose on them. The officer, of course, initially panics, not knowing exactly what to do, but because he is in the padded suit, he is not harmed. The next time, the officer has a better idea of what to do, learning from mistakes he made the first time. By the sixth time the dog has been allowed to attack, the officer's first instinct is not to panic, but rather to remember the training he has had so far and to recall his past experiences. Eventually, if the officer is attacked in the field without the padded suit, the officer can draw off of his experiences and handle the situation in a calmer manner than if he had had no previous experience.

The point of this example is that you need to give your students the chance to gain experience without the fear of getting hurt. In short, you have to provide opportunities for your students to speak in class. Every experience you give them will provide that much more confidence in their ability to publically speak. And just like the police department training, you have to make sure they feel safe. Your classroom needs to feel like a place where mistakes can be made and where students do not have to be perfect. Mistakes are how some of the best lessons are learned.

One way to provide an opportunity for students to speak is to make public speaking a normal part of the class routine. For instance, when running a gifted resource elementary pull-out program, I provided an opportunity every class for a student to speak in public in what was called a "literature circle." During the literature circle, a student presents to the class a book she has read and enjoyed. We set a casual setting with the students putting their chairs in a circle. This way, the speakers did not feel the pressure of the spotlight and were more at ease to present their information. Students were also given guided discussion questions, which they used to create their responses. This way, the presenting students had something to base their performance on. The guided questions made them feel as though they had a support to stand on. The questions were also fairly open-ended and require higher level thinking, so there was not a correct answer per se. (*Note:* The guided questions I used for the literature circle can be found in Appendix A in the back of the book.) The responses were based mostly on the opinions of the students. They just needed to be sure to back up their points of view with examples from the text. This was done to allow students to think at a higher level but also to provide the safety to share opinions and not make the setting too stressful by having a right or wrong answer. Making the setting more relaxed and giving students guidance made the act of public speaking easier to experience.

There are several reasons why the ability to publically speak is so important, but here are a few:
- Public speaking increases self-confidence.
- Public speaking makes you more comfortable around other people.
- Public speaking is one of the most effective ways to get your message across.
- Skills learned through public speaking can boost performance in other areas in life.
- Public speaking allows you to demonstrate your knowledge.

- Public speaking allows you to improve upon your knowledge.
- Public speaking differentiates you in the workplace.
- Public speaking prepares you to be a leader. (Ryan, 2013, para. 5)

When students get out in the real world and are looking for a job, they will likely be competing with thousands of other graduates. What will make someone stand out from all of these people? What will allow potential employers to notice him over the others? The ability to effectively speak in public is an obvious answer.

Using PBA in your classroom will give your students the experience to become more comfortable with public speaking. The more confidence they gain, the better they are going to be at it.

PROBLEM SOLVING

The ability to problem solve is a skill students will use for the rest of their lives. What employer would not want someone who is adept at solving problems? Solving problems saves money and leads to new clients. Although it seems at times like those with the ability to problem solve just have an innate ability to do so, somewhere in their experiences they picked up the skill.

There are ways to teach this in the classroom. Math is an excellent vehicle for problem solving. Attempting to figure out a solution or a formula to use for a particular problem is a method of problem solving. However, with math, there is usually only a single correct answer or one formula that will unlock the solution a student is looking for. It is important to create problem-solving situations where there are numerous possibilities and where students can come up with any number of creative ways to tackle the situation.

I usually will put students in small groups and pay attention to the group dynamics as they are working together. Another part of problem solving is learning how to work with multiple ideas or how to deal with a groupmate who is not contributing.

An important aspect of this problem solving is the time spent reflecting. At the end of a design challenge, I might ask students to reflect upon what worked and what did not. We often say to students that a mistake is not a mistake if you learn from it, but this is something that needs to be taught. How does one learn from a mistake? That is part of the problem-solving process. Why did something not work? What could have been done differently to get a better result? What did you see others doing that might have produced more success?

PROBLEM SOLVING

Problem solving can be used on a much larger scale. Take for instance the following project from my colleague Amy McKibben concerning the Ancient Greeks and Romans.

Secret Mission: Take Over Ancient Greece

The year is 430 B.C. Rome is the rising power in the Mediterranean and has colonial interests in the Greek territory to the east. It is the Roman Senate's dream that one day Rome will control all of the Mediterranean, and Greece is to be the next territory added to the Empire. Students must combine several different skills of research, synthesis, presentation, and others in order to achieve this dream. There is no one answer and there are numerous ways to approach it. Students just need to support their suggestions with research they have uncovered. The ability of students to be able to take a large problem such as this and break it down into smaller, more manageable parts is part of the problem-solving process that will be valuable for students to possess.

You and three or four other young Roman nobles have been carefully chosen to lead an espionage mission into Greece. You are to research the Greek culture and the peninsula as a whole, then report back to the Senate with information that will help to ensure that the military venture and subsequent assimilation of Greece will be a success. This investigation should be a full report on the geography of the region, including visual aids to help the Senate gauge possible takeover routes. You must include a description of the climate of the region, focusing on the ocean's effect on that climate and how it compares to the Roman climate. Additionally, you should create a prototype of Greek advancements in engineering—the Roman Senate is curious about learning about these advancements. Finally, your presentation and report should contain an in-depth account of at least five aspects of Greek culture, including Greek engineering and technology, art and architecture, literature, history, and governance and law. You may wish to include other information, as well, in order to help the Roman Senate fully understand the cultural and geographical implications of this takeover. For example, you might include information about independent city-states, class structure, gender issues, religion, or daily life in order to truly help the Roman Senate learn about this other culture.

When you return from Greece, you are to prepare a presentation before the Senate that outlines the aspects of Greek culture you have discovered and why you feel each aspect is important for the Senate to consider in order to assure the smooth annexation of Greece. You must include any necessary maps, charts, diagrams, pictures, artifacts, models, and any other relevant material. Your presentation must be between 10 and 20 minutes long. The presentation should have a clear argument that explains why each aspect of the culture you describe is important for the Romans to understand as they launch their invasion of Greece.

The Senate will evaluate your presentation on the overall accuracy of your report content, your understanding of the material, and the link you make between the content and its importance to a successful Roman invasion. You will also be provided the opportunity to secretly mark your fellow nobles' contribution to the report and presentation.

Performance-based assessment allows for a lot of different problem-solving scenarios in a lot of different subject areas. It will provide students with a valuable life-long skill that will benefit them in many ways.

COLLABORATION

No matter what the situation, you are going to be working with others at some point in your life. From your coworkers, to your family, to your friends, being able to work with others is a skill that will make these relationships easier to form and maintain. That is why collaboration is such a valuable skill to learn.

It is often a skill we do not teach in the classroom, though. Sure, we put students together for group projects, pair students up to work out a problem, or ask them to help one another. But how much purposeful, guided collaboration takes place in the classroom? When you just throw students together, some things stick, but others do not. Collaboration needs to be taught to students, especially gifted students. Gifted students have a tendency to think they might know everything or that their idea is the best. They need to learn how to listen to others, how to take criticism, and how to deal with it when their idea is not the one chosen.

I learned this mistake the hard way. I was teaching in a gifted program and had just received a fresh batch of fifth graders. Many of these students attended different elementary schools and did not know one another. For the very first project, I had students create multitiered timelines using the song "We Didn't Start the Fire" by Billy Joel. It was a multiweek project I had done with older students that had been very successful. I divided the students into random groups of four and waited for the magic to happen. Instead, I got fireworks—not the good kind. Several of the groups were what could best be described as dysfunctional. Arguments broke out between whose ideas should be used, even when three students saw it one way and one saw it another. Some students worked very hard while others sat back and did nothing. Students would come to me complaining because they brought in their research and another groupmate brought in nothing. I was even getting phone calls and e-mails from parents concerned that some irresponsible child who was not pulling his weight would wreck their child's grade. Even when everyone in the group did work, often one child wanted to dominate the group or wanted the project to be exactly his way without any compromise.

I had made the assumption that if you put a bunch of bright, usually motivated children into a group that they would work well together. Boy, was I wrong. What I learned from this mistake is that you have to teach students how to collaborate so that the group can successfully produce a high-quality product. I will discuss some more specific strategies for collaboration when we get to Chapter 5, but the basics are that students need to be able to find a way to compromise when collaborating. That seems to be the most difficult part for students—they have an idea and are convinced it is the best one and will not budge on it.

One approach I took with students in trying to facilitate successful collaboration was the use of norms. I began by explaining that "norm" was not a person. Norms are expectations that are determined by those directly affected by them. It is important to clarify that these are not rules. Rules are typically set by someone else and because there is no ownership of them, they are so much easier to break. Norms are set by the group and everyone has agreed on them.

I introduced these norms by asking the group or class what they needed from others in order to be successful in a group. These were shared out loud, written down on Post-it notes, discussed at a table, etc. Eventually, these were shared as a whole class. Each norm would be suggested and the class would talk about whether it should or should not be included. For instance, a student might suggest, "Everyone must do an equal amount of work." This is the desire of many gifted students. But is this realistic? If you have four students and each has been given a different task (e.g., one is in charge of making the PowerPoint, another for creating the text for a presentation, etc.), the work may not be divided equally. This norm might need to be reworded so it states, "Everyone does his or her fair share." This gives some flexibility should one task require more time than another.

We eventually created a list of norms as a class or group. Because the students created the list themselves, they had more ownership over it and were more willing to honor the norms. The following is a list of norms one of my sixth-grade classes created:

- You have to cooperate with others.
- Other people's opinions matter.

- Listen.
- Have patience.
- Participate.
- Stay on task.
- Do not dominate the group.

It is important to not forget about the norms. Once they are created, they need to be accessible so that students can regularly refer to them. Going over them again before beginning a group project is often beneficial. Norms can go a long way in enabling successful collaboration when students are working in groups. You will find a brief explanation for creating norms in Appendix A of this book.

Because PBA often takes the form of group projects, being able to collaborate well is going to make for better outcomes. A natural byproduct when students learn to collaborate is that they develop leadership skills. A leader has the confidence to step forward, share ideas, make others feel as though he is listening to their ideas, and to inspire others to accomplish great things. It is an invaluable skill to have for any 21st-century student.

CRITICAL THINKING

Critical thinking is not just being able to problem solve. Critical thinking is being able to think at a higher level. Most teachers are familiar with Bloom's (1956) taxonomy. According to Bloom there are six levels of thinking:
- remembering,
- understanding,
- applying,
- analyzing,
- evaluating, and
- creating.

The first three—remembering, understanding, and applying—are considered lower level thinking skills (Bloom, 1956). Can students recall the capital of Kansas? Can they understand the concept of addition? Can they apply the scientific method to an experiment? We want all students to be able to function at these levels. The challenge to teachers of gifted students is to tap into the higher levels of thinking. Can students analyze a text and infer certain information that is not explicitly there? Can they evaluate a performance they saw and give a clear explanation for what they used as their criteria and how they arrived at their opinion? Can they create something new using the parts and skills of other work?

Using performance-based assessment, we can have students creating, evaluating, and analyzing much more easily than by using a multiple-choice test. Let us consider Figure 1.1, a research paper outline given to third- and fourth-grade students for science:

The first section and part of the second and third sections of the outline ask questions at the remembering, understanding, and applying levels:

- Remembering: Why did you choose this animal?
- Understanding: What is the life cycle of this particular animal?
- Applying: How does the animal's structure relate directly to its survival?

As the outline continues, it begins to build upon these lower level questions. Students are now required to think critically in order to be able to answer the questions:

- Analyzing: What other animals live in or around this exhibit and how do they fit with this animal?
- Evaluating: Did the zoo do a good job of setting up the proper habitat for the animal?
- Creating: What improvements do you think could be made to the habitat to make it better for the animal?

The final performance-based assessment, a research paper, will require students to think critically. This gets them thinking at the higher levels we want gifted students to be tapping into. It would be very difficult to assign the same task and have students think critically using a traditional multiple-choice test.

Besides the obviousness of thinking at a higher level, the advantage of being able to think critically is that students have multiple ideas for the same problem. What employer would not want an employee with that skill? The ability to think critically leads to more ideas, and ideas are what make the world go round.

INFORMATION LITERACY

Trilling and Fadel (2009) define information literacy as the ability to:

- access information efficiently and effectively,
- evaluate information critically and competently, and
- use information accurately and creatively. (p. 65)

This is not only a skill for the classroom—this is a skill for life. If you want to figure out what time to see a movie or where you need to go for your appointment at a new dentist, you will have to figure out where to get this information, how to tell if the information is correct, and how to use the information. Any time you are doing

Introduction
- What is the animal you are studying?
- Why did you choose to learn about this animal?
- What do you hope to learn?

Life Cycle
- What is the primary food of this animal?
- Where does this animal fall on the food chain?
- What is the life cycle of this particular animal?
- Are there animals that existed before this one that it may have evolved from? What leads you to believe this?
- How does the animal's structure relate directly to its survival?

Habitat
- What habitat does the animal live in?
- What about the animal makes this a good habitat to live in?
- What other animals live in this habitat and how does this animal interact with them?
- Do you think this animal could survive in a different habitat?
- How might changes in the animal's habitat be helpful or harmful? Use specific examples.

Observations
- While at the zoo, what did you notice about this animal?
- Did the zoo do a good job of setting up the proper habitat for the animal?
- What improvements do you think could be made to the habitat to make it better for the animal?
- What other animals live in or around this exhibit and how do they fit with your animal?
- Why do you think this animal is a good representative of the habitat the zoo has placed them in?

Conclusion
- How did your research and observations of the animals complement one another?
- What was the most interesting thing you learned about your animal?

Figure 1.1. Research paper outline.

research in the classroom, information literacy will be very valuable. This information can come in the form of print resources or electronic resources.

Performance-based assessment allows students to use information literacy to complete a given project. Research papers, lesson presentations, portfolios, and debates are just a few types of PBA that require information literacy.

Like many others, this is a skill that must be taught purposefully. If we as teachers do not lay the foundation, students will develop their own habits, many of them unproductive. Trying to break a student of a bad habit while teaching her a new one is much more difficult than simply making sure she is applying a skill correctly while learning it for the first time. One mistake we often make as teachers is assuming that students already know how to do something, especially when it comes to Internet research. Depending on what grade we teach, we might assume this has already been taught or that students have been surfing the Internet for years. Making sure students have an understanding of how to properly research both print and electronic resources is not something you should take for granted.

When I work with students for the first time on a PBA that will require them to use literacy skills, I build time into the beginning of the project to cover the basics of how to conduct proper research. For example, if students are required to write a research paper, we work on how to find information in a book using the index, table of contents, or other such areas. We also look at how to put information in our own words. In the age of cut-and-paste, it is common for students to struggle to synthesize information in their own words so that it is not plagiarism. In my own classroom, I have students read passages and put that information in their own words. In addition, I have them properly cite the source so that they learn that skill as well.

In my classroom, if we are just beginning to do research on the Internet, I usually will have students start by doing an Internet scavenger hunt to see how well they can navigate online. Once I assess how competent students are, I keep a careful watch on the ones that did not show much aptitude, making sure they are shown the proper way to conduct a search and how to properly synthesize information.

In the end, the more experience students get with information literacy, the better they are going to become at it. As the teacher, you need to make sure this exposure is guided so that their experiences develop good practices rather than bad habits. Performance-based assessment will allow you to do this.

CREATIVITY AND INNOVATION

The ability to generate ideas leads to creativity and innovation. The more comfortable students become with thinking critically, the more creative their ideas are going to be. There are some who would argue that creativity is something people are born with and cannot be taught. According to Trilling and Fadel (2009), creativity starts with imagination. Because everyone has an imagination, creativity can be fostered and developed. Students just need to be encouraged to do so and given opportunities to display this. You, as a teacher, cannot give students creativity. However, you can certainly create a classroom in which you influence students' ability to be creative. Think of it like a muscle. The more you work it, the stronger it is going to become. If it is not used, however, it will grow weak. If our classrooms focus too heavily on facts, recall, simple skills, and test taking, students will not be ready to think creatively in the real world. As Sir Kenneth Robinson, a thought leader on creativity explained,

"Traditional education's focus . . . has not been good for the development of creativity and innovation. This is changing in the 21st century, and education systems from Finland to Singapore are beginning to put creativity and innovation as a high priority in their desired outcomes for student learning" (Trilling, 2009, p. 57). We need to come up with ways for students to use their creativity in the classroom.

Performance-based assessment is an effective way to allow for this creativity. If students are creating dioramas of ecosystems, they can employ their creativity in the construction. If they are filming a movie trailer that encapsulates a Shakespeare play, they are able to tap into their creativity. If students are debating the merits of the Constitution as an actual delegate of the Constitutional Convention, they can be creative in how they form their arguments and present them.

An easy way to foster creativity in the classroom is to ask open-ended questions. These are questions that do not have a right or wrong answer, but there has to be some thought involved. When working with elementary students in a gifted resource room, I always displayed a small white board with the title "Something to Think About." On this board were questions for students to ponder. Some of the questions I used were:

- If you could have any superpower, what would it be and why?
- Why do ducks walk across the road when they could fly?
- If you were president of the United States, what would be your first act as president?
- Where would you live if you could live anywhere in the world?
- How much wood could a woodchuck chuck if a woodchuck could chuck wood?

The idea behind these questions is that students are exploring their thoughts. By doing so, they are able to create scenarios for themselves and ponder over hypotheticals. This stimulates the imagination and fosters creativity.

Providing students with choice also allows for innovation. If you assign a product for students to create, they are not involved in the innovation of it. If, however, you require them to produce some sort of product of their own choosing, they will have the chance to be creative. An example of this would be a math project concerning volume that I had students do. The final product required that they create a display that demonstrated volume, calculate what the exact volume was, and explain how they arrived at their solution. Some students drew pictures of holes, others drew fish aquariums, while some enterprising students took a physical box and determined the volume of it. I had one student who decided the best place to examine volume was at a swimming pool. She created a model of a swimming pool, complete with diving board, slides, and a kiddie area. She even had various depths of the pool from the diving area to the zero-depth entry, adjusting the volume as she went. She obviously put a lot of thought and creativity into the project because she was given a choice and found inspiration. The more choices we give students, the more chances they have to be creative and innovative.

ADAPTABILITY

Adaptability is one's ability to react to change. An example of this would be the Neolithic Revolution. This is when prehistoric man realized that it was better to farm than it was to hunt. People could stay in one place, feed more people, and specialize in certain jobs. This adaptation to a new way of life did not happen overnight. As a species, it took us several thousands of years to get the concept. Those who were able to adapt later developed civilizations, written languages, and technology. Many of those who were unable to adapt simply died off. The more advanced we become, the more quickly we must adapt to change or get left behind. When we developed automobiles, the world had to adapt to this, building roads and creating new innovations to keep people safe, such as traffic lights and seatbelts. Now we are a nation of drivers.

In the 21st century, we are developing technology at breakneck speed. It does not take more than a year or two to develop the newest technology that renders the old one obsolete. If you have a computer that is more than 5 years old, it most likely is not able to operate the most recent programs. Those who are able to roll with the changes and work with them often find much success. Those who are not able to keep up might find their skill set diminishing. That is why adaptability is such an important skill to have.

How does one teach adaptability in the classroom, though? Using PBA it is quite an easy method. According to Trilling and Fadel (2009):

> The skills involved in flexibility and adaptability can be learned by working on progressively more complex projects that challenge student teams to change course when things aren't working well, adapt to new developments in the project, and incorporate new team members on both current and new projects. (p. 77)

There are a few ways Trillling and Fadel (2009) suggest teaching adaptability, all of which can be accomplished through PBA. The ability to change course when things are not working well plays a role in the collaboration and choice elements of a performance-based assessment. Let us say a group is charged with teaching the class about the Boston Massacre. This is when Boston citizens and British soldiers clashed with one another in 1770 and was a precursor to the American Revolution. The event led to a general distrust of British soldiers and eventually to American independence from the mother country. The group of students chooses to film a reenactment of the incident to show people the perspectives of both the colonists and the British. As they plan for the reenactment, they begin to see the difficulty of pulling off such a feat. From the conflicting schedules of the group members to the lack of availability of prop weapons and costumes, the project is causing more and more stress for the group. The group may be able to find a solution on its own or through conferences with the teacher. The group eventually decides to instead reenact the Boston Massacre using paper bag puppets. So that they do not all have to be together to film the scene, they divide the work up. One creates the paper bag puppets, another writes the scripts, one agrees to film it with help from his brothers, and another is confident she will be able to do the editing with her dad's help. Being able to change the product instead of going forward with one that will result in the assignment being incomplete or poorly executed is an example of adaptability.

Adding new developments to a PBA is a way for teachers to see if students truly understand what it is they are to be learning. It keeps students on their toes and helps them to be more adaptable. An example would be a culminating economics PBA for my eighth graders. On an earlier project, they did a research paper about a career they were interested in doing accompanied by an interview of someone who does that career for a living. Using this career as a basis, I gave students the salary of someone who is just starting out, which they used to develop a monthly budget including food, rent, utilities, etc. They had to create a portfolio with this information, which they then presented to their parents. Students actually had to pick cities where they would be able to partake in their career, find actual apartments, and see how much cars or transportation would cost. While doing this research, I occasionally had them choose "life cards." A life card was something that happened that would affect their budget. Some of the life cards would read:

- Your car needs repairs; subtract $250.
- You are sick. Go to the doctor; subtract $199.
- You need to replace your water heater; subtract $700.
- You worked an extra shift; add $200.

Students then had to adjust their budgets accordingly. When students complained, I explained to them that in life, events occur that are not planned for and that they will need to adapt to certain situations. This is the exact reason people develop savings accounts. Most of the students had not budgeted for a savings account in their original plan but quickly adjusted in case they were given a negative life card.

SELF-DIRECTION

Performance-based assessment lends itself to the use of project-based learning. Students are given a task, they are provided with resources to accomplish this task, and they are given a timeline by which to have the task complete. Projects such as these require a good understanding of time management as well as self-direction. There is much choice provided and students are the ones who determine how they learn. There are many benefits to this approach, one explained here:

> When individuals feel more like origins than pawns, they have higher self-esteem, feel more competent, and perform at higher levels of accomplishment." (Ryan and Grolnick, 1986, p. 551)

The teacher should act more as a coach, guiding from the sidelines and providing resources and guidance when need be. As a result, students are able not just to learn the lesson they are currently working on, but any lesson that comes their way. You create life-long learners, learners who do not need the carrot of a grade or assignment—students who are self-directed.

What employee would not want someone who is self-directed, someone who takes initiative and does not need to be monitored? And what teacher would not want a classroom full of these people? You would be able to do what every teacher's dream is—to actually teach, move around the room and work with students individually, and meet them where their skill levels are at because you do not have to teach to the common denominator of the class.

When you provide students the freedom of self-directed learning, you get such amazing results. Students are more motivated because they have choice in what they do rather than being told what to do. Students can be more creative because they are not constrained by as many requirements. Providing this freedom to students can sometimes be difficult to do as a teacher. Many teachers are so used to being the center of the classroom and directing all of the activities. Performance-based assessment allows the teacher to put the impetus of learning on the student, where it should be.

In order for students to learn self-directedness, you as the teacher need to put certain resources into place so that you are not just throwing them into the deep end of the pool. Three such resources I like to use are contracts, calendars, and rubrics. The purpose of a contract is to keep students focused on the task at hand. If you give them 3 weeks to work on a project, they may very well forget what the main purpose of the project is or what exactly their responsibilities are. The contract acts as a written reminder. It lays out the goals and responsibilities that students can refer to whenever necessary. (*Note:* Examples and reproducibles of blank contracts are in Appendix A.) I always have students complete a contract before they ever touch a project. This causes students to think about what they need or want to accomplish before they simply jump in and start working. It makes their work more purposeful. Only once I have approved a contract by signing it can students begin the project. The contract is also usually signed by the parents. This makes them aware of what their child is doing and better able to help at home if they understand what their child is working on. Figure 1.2 is what a completed contract might look like.

PROJECT CONTRACT

Student Name: Bobby

Project Name: Aquatic ecosystems

Time of Project: 3 weeks

Overall Goal of Project: To understand what animals make up the ocean ecosystem and how they work together and rely on each other.

Skills Learned: Research
               Origami
               Model building

Product of Project: Create a model of an undersea ecosystem with at least 10 origami animals/plants with an explanation of each role in the ecosystem

_____   _____
Student Signature   Teacher Signature

_____
Parent Signature

Figure 1.2. Sample completed contract.

I usually will meet with students or groups periodically through a PBA project. I have them pull out the contract and check to make sure they are living up to the agreement. Because a student created and agreed to the contract, he has ownership over what he is doing. He has not let the teacher down when the project is not where it needs to be—he has let himself down. This is part of learning responsibility, which is a cornerstone of self-direction.

To aid with the time management aspect, I have students create a calendar in which they list tasks and when those tasks should be completed. I have found that without periodic deadlines, students will wait until the last moment to try and do everything. I usually pair the contract and calendar together so that a student has to have both in order for the contract to be signed. This way, when I conferenced with a student, I could refer to the calendar to follow progress. (*Note:* Reproducible blank calendars are in Appendix A.) Table 1.1 is an example of what a calendar might look like for the same project in Figure 1.2.

The calendar causes students to break the project into parts, which is more manageable and helps them to see the steps necessary to complete the project. Students may find that some tasks take much longer than others or that they complete certain ones much more quickly than they originally estimated. For instance, one student might give himself a week to research animals and plants, but it might take him only 3 days. He has left himself only a single day to work on the model when it might take a couple. Adjustments can be made to the calendar and approved by the teacher.

TABLE 1.1

Sample Calendar

Day 1 Research aquatic ecosystems.	Day 2 Research aquatic ecosystems.	Day 3 Research aquatic ecosystems (should be half-way done).	Day 4 Research aquatic ecosystems.	Day 5 Research aquatic ecosystems (have 10 animals/plants chosen).
Day 6 Create two origami animals/plants.	Day 7 Create two origami animals/plants.	Day 8 Create two origami animals/plants.	Day 9 Create two origami animals/plants.	Day 10 Create two origami animals/plants (should have 10 in total).
Day 11 Create a model ecosystem using a clear box and sand.	Day 12 Write index card explanations for three animals/plants.	Day 13 Write index card explanations for three animals/plants	Day 14 Write index card explanations for four animals/plants.	Day 15 Turn in project.

The final piece of this self-directed puzzle is the use of a rubric. We will get into rubrics in far greater detail in Chapter 6, but the basic idea behind them is that the student determines the criteria for which she will be evaluated. This way, the student is completely aware of the expectations because she is the one who set them. A rubric for the ecosystems projects might look like the one in Table 1.2.

This rubric is checked over and approved by the teacher just like the contract and calendar are. The teacher makes sure the rubric measures what the student said he was going to learn in the contract, as well as checks for objectives that are too easy or difficult. Students keep this rubric with them during the entire project so that they are clear on how they are going to be assessed on their performance.

The combination of the contract, calendar, and rubric is one method for teaching self-directedness in students working on PBA.

SUMMARY

This chapter gave several reasons for the inclusion of performance-based assessment in the classroom. In addition to academic and life-long learning skills, PBA can be used to teach specific 21st-century skills. Among these are:

- public speaking,
- problem solving,
- collaboration,

TABLE 1.2

Sample Rubric

Overall	Content/Research	Animals/Plants	Ecosystem
Excellent (A)	1. Index cards have detailed explanations of how each plant/animal fits into the ecosystem. 2. There is a clear picture of how the ecosystem works as a whole. 3. Sources seem to be reliable with complete documentation of where they came from.	1. Has 10 plants/animals from the ocean ecosystem. 2. It is clear what plant/animal is being represented by the origami.	1. Ecosystem looks professional and represents the ocean. 2. Plants and animals are easy to see interacting in the ecosystem. 3. Ecosystem includes many other features besides just the plants/animals.
Good (B–C)	1. The explanations of how each plant/animal fits into the ecosystem are not very detailed. 2. How the ecosystem works as a whole is explained in a basic manner but a clear picture is not provided. 3. Sources seem to be reliable but there is not complete documentation of where they came from.	1. Has seven to nine plants/animals from the ocean ecosystem. 2. It is not always clear which plant/animal is being represented by the origami.	1. Ecosystem represents the ocean but does not look professional. 2. Plants and animals are usually easy to see interacting in the ecosystem. 3. Ecosystem includes a few features besides just the plants/animals but could use more.
Needs Improvement (D–F)	1. Does not have 10 index cards or provides little to no detail of how each plant/animal fits into the ecosystem. 2. How the ecosystem works as a whole is not explained. 3. Sources do not seem reliable or there is no documentation of where they came from.	1. Has six or fewer plants/animals from the ocean ecosystem. 2. Most of the time it is not clear which plant/animal is being represented by the origami.	1. Ecosystem does not seem to represent the ocean or is very sloppy. 2. Plants and animals are not easy to see interacting in the ecosystem. 3. Ecosystem does not include other features besides just the plants/animals.

- critical thinking,
- information literacy,
- creativity,
- adaptability, and
- self-direction.

Any one of the above skills would be a boon for a student to possess. Imagine, however, that you could provide all eight of them for your students. Their Swiss Army knives would be loaded and attractive to employers seeking such innovative individuals. PBA will allow a teacher to expose students to all of these skills and more.

CHAPTER 2

Advantages of Performance-Based Assessment

In the first chapter, we looked at the advantages and skills performance-based assessment provides for students. This chapter will look at the advantages PBA provides for you as the teacher. Here are some examples of these advantages:

- direct observations of student learning,
- good instructional alignment,
- interesting assessments,
- instructional feedback,
- measurement of multiple objectives and concepts,
- active student learning,
- use of higher order thinking skills,
- student interest and empowerment,
- real-world task simulations, and
- authentic assessments.

Let us go through each of these and explain the advantages in more detail.

DIRECT OBSERVATIONS OF STUDENT LEARNING

Performance-based assessment lends itself to self-directed learning. What this means for you as the teacher is that you do not need to be in front of the class controlling all the actions that are taking place. Instead, the students direct the learning and you are able to observe individual students. The advantage of this, of course, is that you can meet students where they are as individuals instead of having to address the class as an entire entity. You will see the individual students who are struggling and be able to react, helping where necessary. You will be able to see where students are having success, enabling you to elevate them to the next level that they are ready to handle. It allows for differentiation within the classroom. There are varying levels of giftedness within a gifted classroom and being able to develop the individual student from where he is rather than developing the class as a single entity allows for much higher achievement results for the individuals.

For example, using direct observation of student learning allows me to have one-on-one conferences with students so that I can truly assess whether they understand the material or not. I will ask them to explain to me what they are working on and what they hope to accomplish. If the students are unable to communicate this clearly, then we have a further discussion on how they can gain an understanding. As mentioned in the introduction, PBA is not just about the end product. It is the process students go through in order to produce the product. This allows you to observe this process up close so that you can see the growth that students are achieving.

GOOD INSTRUCTIONAL ALIGNMENT

Given that many states are turning to the Common Core State Standards to shape their curriculum, and considering that the Common Core are written as action statements, what better way to put these into motion as a teacher than by using performance-based assessments? Here is an example of a Common Core statement in seventh-grade English language arts (National Governors Association Center for Best Practices and Council of Chief State School Officers, 2010a):

> CCSS.ELA-Literacy.RI.7.3: Analyze the interactions between individuals, events, and ideas in a text (e.g., how ideas influence individuals or events, or how individuals influence ideas or events).

This would be quite challenging to be able to demonstrate in an objective multiple-choice assessment. If however, you assigned a performance-based assessment in which the students had to rewrite the story from another character's point of view or create a talk show where they interview people from the book, you'll put this Common Core standard into action. Similarly, here is a Common Core math standard for fifth grade (National Governors Association Center for Best Practices and Council of Chief State School Officers, 2010b):

> CCSS.Math.Content.5.MD.C.5: Relate volume to the operations of multiplication and addition and solve real-world and mathematical problems involving volume.

A teacher could certainly create a problem where students are figuring out the volume of a bathtub in a written problem, but wouldn't it be so much more significant and meaningful to the students if you brought in an actual object or a model bathtub and gave them the challenge of determining the volume? You'd add the additional challenge of not having a perfectly rectangular object or tub. By making the problem performance based, students have to factor in the curvature of the object, the possible varying depths, and other real-world problems we often cannot capture on a piece of paper.

INTERESTING ASSESSMENTS

This goes without saying, but interesting assessments are what performance-based assessment is all about: giving students the opportunity to be creative while having them analyze and synthesize information that allows them to solve real-world problems. (*Note:* Several interesting assessment examples are provided in Chapter 4.)

In addition, by giving students a choice in how they are assessed, it allows them to play to their strengths as well as be creative. For my fifth-grade science class, students were allowed to choose how they demonstrated what they learned. I gave them 10 performance-based assessment suggestions such as portfolios, presentations, and essays. For those students who were a little more traditional, I gave them the option of a multiple-choice test, but adapted it to be a performance-based assessment: The students had to create the multiple-choice test themselves, complete with an answer key.

One student taught the class about light and sound through an interactive museum she created. She set up five stations, one for each of the learning objectives. At each station was a tri-fold that explained the objective in simple terms, using lots of examples and visuals, much like a real museum exhibit. She also had a hands-on demonstration so that students were able to put the concept into action for a more memorable lesson. At one of the stations, she had a glass of water and a pencil to demonstrate refraction. At another she built a device that had various widths and lengths of guitar string. Based on these variations, students could see how vibrations affect pitch. Yet a third exhibit had students creating a coloring page of the various forms of light and the benefits that each serves. Just like a museum curator, she moved around the room, helping people with the exhibits, and rotated the groups regularly so that all had a chance to participate in each activity.

Another student created a video game as a demonstration of physical and chemical change. This made me a little cautious at first but when I saw what he was demonstrating, I knew students would remember the content far longer than if they had read about it in a book or done a worksheet. The student created a quest for a knight to slay a dragon. At each stage of the quest, the knight had to determine whether he was encountering a physical or chemical change. There was a part where the knight fought an ice princess, and the player of the game had to determine whether the frozen ice was a physical or chemical change. The culmination of the video game was a battle against the dragon. The player had to figure out whether the fire the dragon breathed was a physical or chemical change and then had to use the opposite change to defeat the dragon. As a class, we determined that the burning was a chemical change, so we cut the dragon with a sword (a physical change), winning the game, learning a lifelong lesson, and mastering the intended concept.

These were interesting assessments that I would have never created on my own as a teacher, but that were very memorable. Giving your students choice will produce amazing things because they are creative. The advantage for the teacher, of course, is that these assessments are so much more interesting to grade and exciting to see what possibilities students will come up with.

INSTRUCTIONAL FEEDBACK

Providing instructional feedback on a multiple-choice test is not the easiest thing to do. Aside from a "great job" or a "need to study more" scrawled at the top of the test, the feedback is limited because the range of thinking on an objective multiple-choice test is limited. There is only one correct answer and a student either does or does not get it correct, and there is not much for the instructor to glean about the student's knowledge or skillset.

Performance-based assessment allows for much more instructional feedback. In fact, it only works effectively with lots of it. When evaluating a performance, the teacher might see instances of success and instances of needed improvement within the same action. Because of this, the teacher must provide ample instructional feedback for the student to be able to learn from what she has done. This feedback can be written at the end of a research paper or in periodic spots on a rubric. It could be oral feedback, given by sitting down with a student and conferencing on her performance. Whatever the method, it is important that the feedback be structured to enable the student to improve and build upon her performance for the next time.

I am sure this has happened to all of us at one time or another in our academic career: You turn in a paper and when you get it back, written at the top of the page is an A with "excellent work" or "well done" written, but nothing else. You would think you would be satisfied with an A. But you are not; you want to know *why* you got the A. What did you do to deserve the A so that you can repeat it and get a similar result next time? How are you to learn if you do not know what you did right? We often are told we learn from our mistakes. We can also learn from what we do well. Not providing any feedback is excusable only with a multiple-choice assessment.

When using PBA the teacher needs to be prepared to offer lots of feedback, even when the student has mastered a skill. This feedback should not just be general praise, it should be specific so the student can see what he did well and what he needs to work on. For example, a student is given the task of linking the five themes of geography to one of the original 13 colonies. You provide a rubric for the student to make him aware of the expectations. The student gives a presentation in order to communicate what he learned, which is evaluated on the rubric. Rather than just circling the appropriate rubric description, you need to be sure to explain *why* you circled the categories you did and explain what the student did to earn that distinction or what he needs to do next time to get a higher grade. It might look something like the rubric in Figure 2.1.

Instructional feedback does require more time from the teacher. Sure, it would be great to run 30 multiple-choice tests through the Scantron machine in one minute rather than spend a half hour grading each of those tests in essay form. Sometimes your efforts do not feel appreciated when the student looks only at the grade, ignoring the scads of comments you made, and then pitches it in the wastebasket. Ultimately, however, it is what is best for kids to learn, and that is what we are in the business of doing. One thing I do to ensure students clearly understand why they received the grade they did is to conference with them about their assessment. While the class is working on the next PBA, this gives the teacher the opportunity to talk one-on-one with students about their previous assessment. Most times, students are already aware of their deficiencies and where they can improve quality. Conferencing allows for self-reflection from the students and a growing awareness of why they receive the grades they do.

MEASUREMENT OF MULTIPLE OBJECTIVES AND CONCEPTS

On a multiple-choice test, each question measures one objective or concept. This means the objectives and concepts must be clearly separated into various parts. You never get to see them combined as they usually are in the real world. In reality, when we are performing an activity, we are engaged in multiple objectives and concepts.

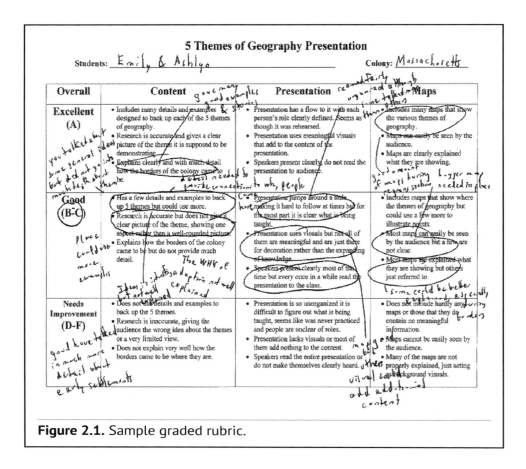

Figure 2.1. Sample graded rubric.

Very rarely in real life are we breaking activities down to single skills that we do in a specific order. For instance, just think of getting dinner ready. This in itself is problem solving. Typically, you are not just making one thing. You might have a roast in the crock pot, bread in the oven, noodles on the stovetop, and green beans in the micro-wave. Each one of these items is prepared and cooked differently. In addition, the table needs to be set, drinks poured, and the family gathered. You are doing multiple tasks to solve the problem of preparing dinner. If you broke the process down and only did one of these tasks at a time, it would take half a day to get dinner ready. Most real-world problems involve multitasking.

Performance-based assessment prepares students for this real-world skill. As the teacher, you can focus on several skills in a single product. This way, multiple objectives and concepts can be covered. An example of this would be the performance-based assessment in Figure 2.2.

The project in Figure 2.2 culminates in a single day when speeches are presented, campaigns are unveiled, and commercials are shown. Even though the focus seems

CREATING YOUR OWN POLITICAL PARTY

For this assignment you will create your own political party. Like all political parties, you need to develop a platform that displays your collective beliefs. This platform will eventually be displayed in a speech that the candidate you choose will give. The first step is to determine where your party fits on the political spectrum.

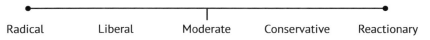

| Radical | Liberal | Moderate | Conservative | Reactionary |

From there you must decide on the issues your party will support and where they stand. Some examples are:

- Taxes
- Foreign Affairs
- Environment
- Defense Spending
- Health Care
- Social Security/Unemployment
- Education
- Civil Rights
- Immigration
- Economy

The project includes:

1. Speech
   - The candidates, with their speechwriters, will write a speech they will deliver at the caucus. This speech should convey the major parts of the party's platform.
   - The speech will be evaluated mostly on content but also on presentation, so choose a candidate you feel is a good speaker.
   - Both vice presidential and presidential candidates will give speeches.

2. Campaign
   - You'll need to come up with a campaign slogan and create posters touting this slogan.
   - You'll need to create a mascot that represents the party.
   - You'll need to film a 30-second commercial representing your platform.

3. Preparation
   - The political parties should nominate their candidates and form their platform.
   - The candidates will write their speeches.
   - Elect a campaign manager to run the party's campaign. There should be *no* negative campaign posters, commercials, or slogans. The objective is to make your party look good, not to insult or tear down the other parties.
   - The day of the caucus, candidates will be introduced at the podium. The vice-presidential candidates will go first and give their speech. The presidential nominees will follow. In the speeches, the parties' platforms should be established.

Figure 2.2. Sample PBA that covers multiple objectives.

to be on political parties, there are several 21st-century skills being assessed, some of which are:

- public speaking (i.e., performing the speech itself),
- problem solving (i.e., deciding how the party will stand on each of the issues),
- collaboration (i.e., working as a group to create a political party),
- critical thinking (i.e., thinking how these stances will be perceived by the public and how the group/party will convey this message in a speech),
- information literacy (i.e., researching the various issues to gain an understanding of them), and
- creativity (i.e., creating the campaign posters and commercial).

Projects such as these allow for several concepts and/or objectives to be measured. The key to doing so is having a well-written rubric, which we will discuss in more detail in Chapter 6.

ACTIVE STUDENT LEARNING

If you have set up your PBA correctly, students are going to be doing more of the teaching than you will. Whether it is conducting the research, creating the product, or even directly teaching the class, the students will be active participants. They are not simply the recipients of information as is the case in many traditional classrooms. Instead, they are the ones driving the cart. This is a huge advantage to the teacher, as she is not going to have to be responsible for everything that goes on in the classroom.

One method I use to achieve maximum active student learning is having the class teach a unit. When my class did a unit concerning the American Revolution, I began by giving the students a little background information. I did this through a series of lectures designed to give students an overview of all of the main events and people of the Revolution. Students took notes and listened for events and people that sounded interesting to them. Once I finished, I had the students write down the three events or people they would be most interested in learning more about. Based on their interest, I grouped students together. Students filled out a contract that looked something like Figure 2.3.

We created the essential question in Figure 2.3 as an entire class and I assigned the due date. The group was responsible for creating learning outcomes. I taught them to start with lower level thinking—simple objectives that build up to higher level, complex objectives. They looked something like Figure 2.4. Figure 2.4 starts with the basic information of "what" and "who" and then gets into higher levels of thinking such as "why" and "what if." Then the group determined how they were going to teach the class these learning objectives, as shown in Figure 2.5.

Project Topic: Boston Massacre

Essential Question: What role did this person/event play in shaping the American Revolution?

Due Date of Project: December 15

Learning Outcomes *(at least three)*:

Product of Project:

_____   _____
Student Signature   Teacher Signature

_____
Parent Signature

Figure 2.3. Sample project contract.

LEARNING OUTCOMES *(LIST AT LEAST THREE.)*:

1. What was the Boston Massacre?
2. Who were the main people involved?
3. Why did this cause tension between Britain and the colonists?
4. Would the American Revolution have occurred if the Boston Massacre had not?

Figure 2.4. Sample learning outcomes.

PRODUCT OF PROJECT

The presentation will be broken down into three parts:

1. A PowerPoint and re-enactment providing the basics of who, what, when, and where.
2. A class discussion on the comparison between the woodcarving of the Boston Massacre by Paul Revere and another, less biased retelling of the event.
3. A debate between group members on whether the American Revolution would have happened without the Boston Massacre to fuel it.

Figure 2.5. Sample presentation outline.

As you can see, this lesson is very active in that the students have to become experts on their topic in order to be able to teach it to the class. In my own experience, by having the students teach what they have learned to others, the retention rate tends to be about 90% as compared to less than 10% when I simply give students my original lecture. Students are not only actively learning, but they are retaining what they learned at a very high rate. This is something teachers wish for all their students.

HIGHER ORDER THINKING SKILLS

Performance-based assessment lends itself to higher order thinking skills, a must-have in gifted classrooms. Because students are asked to creatively problem solve, they have to tap into higher levels of thinking. This is good for you as the teacher because the expectations for gifted students is becoming increasingly challenging. In many states, teachers are expected to help their students surpass a year's worth of content and skills, sometimes more. Theoretically, this means if a seventh grader comes into your class at a seventh-grade level of math, you need to develop her skills and knowledge enough to be able to handle the eighth-grade material when she is an eighth grader. The added challenge for many of those in gifted education is that if a seventh grader comes to you and is advanced enough to be learning math at a ninth-grade level, that means you need to foster enough growth so she can handle 10th-grade math as an eighth grader. The debate that rages on in the gifted community is whether already-advanced students can advance even further, or whether that growth will eventually plateau. I personally do not believe there is a ceiling on growth, as long as higher level thinking skills are sufficiently employed. One way to advance students in any subject area is to provide lessons and assessments that involve higher level thinking skills. This breaks the limit that lower level questions can sometimes put on learning.

The benefits of higher level thinking skills are many. Higher level thinking should:

- improve information retention,
- enhance problem-solving skills,
- increase creativity, and
- elevate standardized test scores.

You probably recognize a few of the 21st-century skills from the last chapter, not to mention the always-important benefit of elevating standardized test scores. Research shows there is a link between higher level thinking skills and increased student achievement in the classroom. In one study conducted by the National Assessment of Educational Progress (NAEP), assessments were given to a cross-range of students. These assessments were derived from representative samples of students in fourth, eighth and 12th grades throughout the United States. In his study of these test scores, Harold Wenglinsky found that teaching critical thinking is associated with higher test scores (Wenglinsky, 2000; 2002; 2003). Wenglinsky went on to state that "Instruction emphasizing advanced reasoning skills promotes high student performance" (Wenglinsky, 2004, p. 32).

This seems like common sense. If a student can analyze, evaluate, or create, he can remember, understand, and apply. Because students can understand the concept or skill at a higher level of thinking, they can do more things with these concepts and skills than if they just understood them at a lower level. What teacher of gifted would not want that for his students?

STUDENT INTEREST AND EMPOWERMENT

By teaching your students to learn, you have given them control of their own education. This is extremely empowering. Students are no longer dependent on someone else to provide their education. They have a say in what they are learning, how they are learning it, and how they demonstrate their new skills.

The best way to get students' interest and empower them is by giving them as much choice as possible. Young people often do not have much choice. Adults—be they parents, coaches, or teachers—decide most things for them. However, when you give students choice, their learning experiences open up to all sorts of interesting possibilities. When I taught sixth-grade science, I set up the classroom to provide total student choice. I put up the entire year's curriculum on a bulletin board broken down into six units. There were rocks, physical/chemical changes, cells, reproduction, energy, and light/sound. All that was on this board were the objectives that needed to be covered, word for word. To up the ante a little bit, I included one or two additional objectives that were from a higher grade level. It looked something like Figure 2.6. The italicized objectives were the ones above grade level. I told students they had the entire year to learn all of the content standards listed on the board. How they learned and demonstrated this information was completely in their hands. In order to model the structure, we worked on a mini-project together to provide a basic understanding of what a self-directed product should look like.

The students were given 10 choices for how they would show what they learned, all of them performance-based assessments. The choices were:

- demonstration,
- electronic portfolio,
- essay,
- exhibition,
- journal,
- research paper,
- presentation,
- portfolio,
- performance, and
- student-created test.

I showed students projects from past years as examples so that students could see with their own eyes what the possibilities were. Once students had a good idea of how the structure for the class worked, I turned all choice over to them.

Using the contract, calendar, and rubric scenario shared before, students chose how they learned the content, the due dates, and the expectations by which they were evaluated. My classroom most always consisted of 20 students working independently on 20 different projects. Some students were working on the same topics, but they

---

CHEMICAL AND PHYSICAL CHANGES

- Explain that in a chemical change, new substances are formed with different properties than the original substance (e.g., rusting, burning).
- Explain that in a physical change (e.g., state, shape, and size), the chemical properties of a substance remain unchanged.
- Explain that chemical and physical changes occur all around us (e.g., in the human body, cooking, and industry).
- *Demonstrate that chemical changes can happen over a series of steps.*

Figure 2.6. Curriculum broken up into standards and objectives.

---

were at different places or producing different products. My role as the teacher was to provide the resources students needed, whether it was books, laptops with Internet access, supplies to conduct experiments, or anything else needed to get the work done. I periodically met with students individually to monitor their progress or encourage them if they were stuck. In most cases, I found students were exactly where they needed to be or even better, and I was only getting in their way.

This approach was a little scary at first, but I was pleasantly surprised by the amount of quality work I received from students. Most students really enjoyed the independence and choice afforded to them. There were even some that finished with their projects before the school year was up and moved on to independent enrichment projects; they chose what they wanted to learn about and created their own learning objectives. I received projects concerning baseball, roller coasters, earthquakes, birds, evolution, volcanoes, and weather. These projects tended to be even more in depth than the ones students had to do for class, even though there were no grades involved. At that point, students did not care about grades because they were very passionate about what they were learning about.

There were a couple of students who did not do well with the independence, who were so used to having decisions made for them that they were uncomfortable making them for themselves. Together we were able to modify the lessons to make them more structured and students were able to find success. In the end, I had over 60 students take part in science in this manner and all of them were able to finish the projects for the year and earned either advanced or accelerated scores on the state tests that year. As a bonus, students felt empowered to work on independent research projects of their own and were interested in learning about science because they had complete control.

REAL-WORLD TASK SIMULATIONS

In the real world, tasks are almost always PBAs. Scientists, mathematicians, engineers, and researchers don't take tests, but actually create new theories, products, and ideas. This is what performance-based assessment in the classroom allows you as the teacher to provide for the students—the opportunity to create. In addition to that, students perform real-world tasks. This allows you to reach a higher level of rigor and relevance. This higher level includes skills such as analysis, synthesis, evaluation, and the application of a real-world situation. This would be very difficult to achieve with an objective multiple-choice test.

For instance, take a nationally recognized program like Invention Convention. Invention Convention has students create an invention that solves a problem. Then, the students must design and create a model of the invention to show how it works. Along the way, the students might run into all sorts of real-world problems such as how to build the invention, what materials should be used, and whether the invention has already been invented. For each of these real-world questions, the student must modify, adapt, and overcome the unpredictable situation following the STEM design process. Once the students have figured out their invention, the final product has to be presented to a judge who evaluates the invention's merits and students' clarity of communication. Presenting to the judge puts this performance-based assessment into real-world and unpredictable situations. The students do not know what questions the judge may ask. They have to be ready for anything just as one would have to be when presenting something for one's job. Throughout this process, students are also employing lots of real-world, 21st-century skills such as problem solving, information literacy, creativity, and presentation.

It is very easy to simulate real-world situations using PBA, such as inviting outside evaluators, using technology to bring in experts to the classroom, presenting a problem that solves a real problem in the community, or participating in a national program that has a set criteria that will be evaluated. All of these require the student to problem solve at a higher level of thinking.

AUTHENTIC ASSESSMENTS

As a teacher, one of my greatest frustrations is that even if I spend months covering a concept, there are students who will forget it no sooner than I stop talking about it. Having ideas and lessons that are "sticky" is a key to enduring understanding. The more authentic an assessment is, the more memorable and meaningful it will be to the student. Do you ever look back on your school career and think to yourself, "I remember that one time in class when I was filling in a bubble on a Scantron . . ."? Or do you remember the moments when you were involved in some sort of performance-based assessment? There is one such moment for me from my primary education days that stands out. When I was in first grade, we had to design a structure that would allow us to drop an egg from a third-story building and not break. This was certainly a PBA. The egg either did or didn't break. I remember watching the attempts of my classmates and observed how when one was successful, others turned to their contraption and made adjustments accordingly. Similarly, when an egg ended up a fatality on the asphalt, we would make changes so that our egg did not suffer the same fate. It was memorable to me because it was authentic. We were not reading about other students doing this, or simulating it in a story problem, or even watching a video of it. We were engaged in the actual process of problem solving. Although I have never been required to create a device that would spare an egg in the last 30 years, I have certainly used the 21st-century skills we employed that day: creativity, problem solving, creative thinking, and adaptability.

Authentic moments for me as a teacher are the ones when students come to visit 3, 5, or sometimes even 10 years later and say to me, "I remember when we did this in your class." The one I probably hear about the most involved an authentic simulation concerning prehistoric people. For years I taught a lesson on the development of prehistoric people in which students would read a chapter of the textbook that focused on such developments as fire, language, religion, leadership, farming, shelter, etc. Students would read about these and then we would have a discussion, which always seemed to come out flat. Students just were not getting how important these ideas were and how they led to the advancement of human civilization. They took them for granted because they are everyday occurrences. I tried strengthening the lesson by having them read an article in *Newsweek* rather than just a textbook chapter that would get them to think about it at a much higher level. Still, with the lifeless and uninspired discussion, student interest was dim. Finally, I decided I would put them in bands of people and have them pick from a list of 10 advancements, only three of which they were allowed to use. For instance, if they left language off of their list, they were not able to talk. If they left farming, hunting, and domestication off the list, they would starve to death. They had to really consider what would be important for survival and what they could live without. After making their decisions, I took the students out into the woods behind the school and let them fend for themselves like the prehistoric people had to. During these 45 minutes, they had to create a mini-civilization and try to survive. I would come around and throw challenges at them like a saber-toothed tiger attack, or the ice age happening, or some other real-world issue prehistoric people might have faced. They could combine as bands or even try to simulate an attack against one another.

When we came back into the classroom at the end of the simulation, I could not keep the students from talking about what had gone on. What strategies seemed to work? What advancement could they have used that they left off their list? How might they have done things differently? I suddenly had them engaged in the discussion because it was something that had really happened to them, not to a group of people millions of years ago. This made the lesson authentic to them and as a result, they cared about it. Nothing they read about in a book or article or that they would have answered on a test would have provided this experience. Only the authentic activity was able to get them there.

This is what PBA can do for your classroom. Whether it is a science, math, language arts, or social studies lesson, by making the lesson authentic, you can guarantee yourself a more enduring lesson that students will talk about even when all the other facts, formulas, and philosophies have faded away.

SUMMARY

Performance-based assessment makes your job easier and allows you to do what so many teachers have found it a challenge to do in the No Child Left Behind era of assessment and accountability—to be able to teach. You can make meaningful connections to your students, and they will be able to make meaningful connections to the skills you are teaching.

CHAPTER 3

Types of Performance-Based Assessment

I hope the first two chapters have convinced you of the benefits to using PBA in the classroom. The next logical question is: What types of performance-based assessments are there? There are many choices when it comes to this, possibly hundreds. This chapter will focus on 10 types of performance-based assessment:

- oral presentations,
- debates/speeches,
- role playing,
- group discussions,
- interviews,
- portfolios,
- exhibitions,
- essays,
- research papers, and
- journals/student logs.

For each one of these, I will describe what the PBA looks like and the pros and the cons to using it.

ORAL PRESENTATIONS

So much about what a student knows can be expressed in an oral presentation. I am sure you have had this type of student in your class, the type that raises his hand and can provide insightful, meaningful responses when taking part in discussion, but as soon as you ask that same student to write down his thoughts, you are lucky to get a one- or two-word written response. He is not able, or more likely, not willing, to give you the same insightful responses in writing. In dealing with these kinds of students, the question for me became: Why couldn't this student provide his answers orally, especially if it meant getting responses like I did in class? The next time I had a test, I offered such a student the alternative of going in the back room and recording his responses on a tape recorder. Sure enough, instead of the short responses devoid of detail, I got long responses that showed a true understanding of what the student knew and at a deeper level of thinking, no less. I know there are a lot of language arts teachers bristling at this suggestion, saying to themselves, "But students have to learn how to express themselves through writing." I completely agree. After the student had recorded his answers on the tape recorder, I then asked him to play back the response and write it out as a transcript, but to leave out the "umms," "ahhs," and "likes." The result was a fairly detailed essay that I would not have gotten from the student otherwise. The student had this in himself the entire time; I just needed to figure out a way to get it out of him. On the flip side are those students who do not know how to express themselves in an oral presentation and the acquisition of the skill is very valuable for them.

What It Looks Like

Oral presentations can take several forms, but they typically consist of an informative speech whose primary purpose is audience education. Some of the forms can be:

- an individual or group report,
- an oral briefing,
- an oral exam,
- a panel discussion, or
- an oral critique.

The student's goal in an oral presentation is to verbally teach classmates what she has learned after researching a particular topic or skill. A successful oral presentation needs to be set up just like an essay would, with a topic sentence, supporting detail, and several drafts before the final presentation. This structure is something that should be taught to students. This can be done with modeling, looking at exemplary examples of great oral presentations, or practicing presentations with no consequences.

Pros

- Oral exams are an instant method for conveying information. In a written response, only the reader benefits from the insight and information, but in an oral presentation, anyone listening in the audience receives the benefit as well.

- Sometimes it is so much easier to explain something verbally than to try and capture it in writing. Oral presentations allow students to display a high level of understanding. It also allows you as the teacher to push a student to achieve a higher level of thinking. If a student is explaining himself and seems on the cusp of a truly insightful comment, you as the teacher can provide a prompt or follow-up question that allows the student to access that.

- There is a certain amount of transparency involved in an oral presentation. Even a smooth-talking student is going to have difficulty faking his way through a presentation without some substance. The added pressure of presenting in front of people provides additional motivation to do a good job. If you fail on a written test, the failure is private between only the student and the teacher. An oral presentation provides a certain amount of accountability in that the student does not want his failure to be seen by everyone, so he will be more motivated to present well.

- Oral communication is a two-way street. The speaker and the audience comprise two separate aspects of an oral presentation. The audience may add insights and prompt the speaker to be clearer, to go further into an explanation, or to bounce an idea into further discussion. Although the presenter is the one who is supposed to be doing the teaching, an attentive and insightful audience can provide some learning for the presenter as well. As the teacher, you are also able to provide instant feedback and suggestions for improvement.

Cons

- Oral presentations can be time consuming. You can have 30 students write an essay all at the same time, and if each student takes 15 minutes to explain him or herself, it is only costing you 15 minutes of class time. If, however, 30 students are each giving that same 15 minutes of information in an oral presentation, each has to go one at a time. It could take a couple of class days to get through each student.

- Oral presentations can be stressful for students. There are some students who would rather fail the assignment than have to present in front of the class.

- Oral presentations can be tricky to grade at times. Because the information is coming quickly, there is no opportunity to go back and review what was said. Some teachers choose to videotape oral presentations so they have the ability to view it several times to make sure nothing is missed.

DEBATES/SPEECHES

This is another form of oral presentation, but instead of seeking to inform, the main goal is to persuade. The presentation is elevated up to a higher level of thinking because it doesn't just convey information but employs tactics to convince someone that one student's opinions or viewpoints are more valuable than another's. It is a process more complicated than the usual presentation because it looks at "ethos, the credibility of the speaker; logos, the logical proof and reasoning presented in the words of the speech; and pathos, the use of emotional appeals to influence the audience" (Brydon & Scott, 2000).

What It Looks Like

Debates are especially great to use when the concept being taught is ambiguous or allows for multiple perspectives. When I was teaching the Civil War, rather than tell the students about the many differences and issues that split the country in two, I had them take sides on a particular issue, provided them with primary documents as resources, and then gave them a format to structure their debate. This required them to gain an understanding of the issue, both sides of the argument, and why each side would take the perspective it did. Students participated in debates on state versus federal rights, slavery, executive power, the Emancipation Proclamation, the failure of Reconstruction, and other topics. We even used the Lincoln-Douglas debate format, shown in Figure 3.1.

Speeches are another form of this persuasive oral presentation. While delivering a speech, the student is either playing a role or representing a political party/candidate. He must convince people of his platform or ideals. Although not as interactive as a debate, the speech still requires the student to tap into higher levels of thinking and make a sound argument.

Pros

- Typically, debates/speeches are fun. The process can be competitive, which can act as an additional motivation for students.
- They promote collaboration. Debates are usually done in teams. The team must work together in order to present a unified argument. Any breaks in consistency will only weaken the argument, so the group must plan and present together.
- There is a certain degree of analysis involved. Students must look at a problem and find the best way to present their side. They must pull the right information to make their argument and anticipate what the other side will argue as well.

Affirmative Constructive: 5 minutes
Team Conference: 2 minutes
Cross-Examination of Affirmative: 5 minutes
Negative Construction: 5 minutes
Team Conference: 2 minutes
Cross-Examination of Negative: 5 minutes
Team Conference: 2 minutes
1st Affirmative Rebuttal: 4 minutes
Team Conference: 1 minute
Negative Rebuttal: 6 minutes
Team Conference: 1 minute
2nd Affirmative Rebuttal: 3 minutes

Figure 3.1. Lincoln-Douglas debate format.

- Students must have good research skills in order to include information that supports their opinion. The argument becomes so much more concrete and persuasive when there are facts or data to back it up.
- Students also must think on their feet. If students are involved in a cross-examination or must construct a rebuttal based on what the other team is stating, students need to be able to quickly extemporate. Students have to understand both sides of an argument in order to be able to argue their own because they must develop counterarguments. This also involves having good listening and note-taking skills.

Cons

- Debates/speeches can cause tension within a class. Because you are pitting classmates against other classmates, the emotions that run with trying to make an argument and make the other side look "bad" can carry over socially.
- Those students who are more confident and capable may dominate those students who have less confidence. As the teacher, you will want to be mindful to pit students against each other who are of similar ability. Otherwise, you could have a massacre on your hands and the students without much confidence will not have time to or will be too intimidated to participate to their full potential.
- The students might get stuck debating something they are diametrically opposed to. This can make them shut down or refuse to participate. Although it is good for students to explore opinions they do not agree with, you have to be careful not to offend students who have a strong belief system, such as a religiously based one.

ROLE PLAYING

This is a form of creative oral presentation where a student must inhabit a specific persona and carry out the role from that person's perspective. It allows students to walk a day in the shoes of someone else and helps them to understand different perspectives. A constant struggle with students is to get them to think about anything from another perspective than their own. Giving them opportunities to explore other perspectives will allow them to gain a better understanding of a character, time period, or idea.

What It Looks Like

Role playing can involve having a person assume the role of a character from a novel to demonstrate how he would react to situations the character had to experience. Or it can involve a mock trial in which a student is given a specific role to play such as a lawyer, a witness, a defendant, the judge, or even the jury. Although a student is focusing in on her specific role, she is getting an understanding of how a trial works and of the arguments being made. When I taught about the Articles of Confederation, rather than give students a dry overview of the content, I assigned each student in the class to be an actual Founding Father who participated in the Constitutional Convention. The students were required to role-play an individual (I provided them with a one-page background on the person to provide some context) and make an argument that this person made at the actual Convention. Through these role-playing activities, students learned the many arguments made at the Convention as well as why the Articles of Confederation failed. Students got the exact same information they could have gotten from a book or from me presenting it to them, but they got to have the fun of playing a character and trying to understand why the Founding Fathers made the arguments they did.

Pros

- Role playing makes students more empathetic to a situation. Young people often have difficultly relating to other perspectives or situations that are not their own. Role playing makes it easier for them to try and imagine what it would be like to be a different person, be in a different time, or to have a different perspective.
- Students get to be creative while playing a role. Some of the quietest students make the best role players because they get to be someone else. Their inhibitions that prevent them from being more active in class fall by the wayside.

- Role playing encourages the use of critical thinking. Students must analyze and solve a problem not from their own perspective, but from what they understand about another perspective.
- Role playing makes a real-world connection. Students envision their decisions in the context of their assigned character and the real world. Anything you can do in the classroom to make a real-world connection is always going to be a good thing.
- Students get to play an active part in the lesson. Role playing allows students to make decisions. Even though the decisions are supposed to be coming from the perspective of the person they are playing, they still have some determination in what goes on in the lesson, which can be hugely empowering for students.

Cons

- Students need background information in order to understand their character. Even when presented with an opportunity to play a different character, students still make decisions based on their own perspective if they haven't done sufficient research, which can cause the lesson to be lost.
- It can cause embarrassment for students. This tends to be the case if a male student is asked to play the role of a girl or vice-versa. There can also be the challenge of a student being asked to play a role they do not like. This often happens when a student has to play a villain.

GROUP DISCUSSIONS

Discussions can take what is being learned and elevate it to a higher level. There are two types of group discussions. One involves students participating and answering with very surface-level responses. The discussion dies on the vine before it can bloom. It looks like a discussion, but it certainly does not feel like one. There is usually no energy, no passion to the discussion, and although you might get the information you seek from students, there is no depth. The second type of group discussion is one in which students cannot wait to participate because what they want to share is burning a hole in their mind. It may require some content knowledge, but it also requires tapping into experiences and opinions. This is the type of discussion you want to have in your classroom.

What It Looks Like

An easy way to make a group discussion meaningful is to make sure the questions being asked are higher level questions. If you are looking for discussions to generate close-ended, knowledge-based information, it becomes a hunt-and-peck event where you are simply looking for someone to provide the correct answer. If, however, the questions are open-ended, higher level questions designed to be cracked open and explored, the discussion will be meaningful. Some of this involves preparing challenging, higher level questions ahead of time. This also means being able to generate these higher level questions in response to what a student has said. It requires a teacher to be able to think quickly on her feet and ask appropriate follow-up questions to mine all the meaningful lessons from a conversation.

One method for getting meaningful group discussions is the use of the Socratic Method. This was a method developed by the Greek philosopher Socrates designed to arrive at a certain truth. The basic concept behind it is that no matter what the response to a question is, it's followed up by another question. Figure 3.2 is an example of the Socratic Method adapted from a third-grade lesson by math teacher Rick Garlikov (2014). Generally, there are three types of questions:

1. Opening questions generate discussion at the beginning of the seminar in order to elicit themes.
2. Guiding questions help deepen and elaborate the discussion, keeping contributions on topic and encouraging a positive atmosphere and consideration for others.
3. Closing questions lead participants to summarize their thoughts and learning and personalize what they've discussed. (Mangrum, 2010, p. 44)

Each question is designed to have the students digging a little deeper than lower level questions would. In Figure 3.2, notice the teacher starts off with some lower level questioning to warm students up. If the teacher just started with the higher level questions, it might have been more challenging for students to generate higher level responses.

Group discussions do not need to be led by the teacher. Teachers often feel the need to be the ones steering the ship so that it will head in the direction they want it to go in, but sometimes the most interesting trips involve detours. In this case, allowing the discussion to wander to seemingly unrelated topics or to allow students to explore ideas you had not even considered might actually produce better results than you expect. Dividing the students into groups and providing them with a few guiding questions to get the discussion going can lead to such a thing. Without the teacher there, students might provide more creative answers instead of searching for the answer they believe the teacher is looking for.

TEACHER: How many is this? [*Teacher holds up 10 fingers.*]
STUDENTS: 10.
TEACHER: Who can write that on the board? [*Most students' hands go up.*]

> *A student writes 10 with digits: 10*

TEACHER: Who can write 10 another way? [*Not as many hands go up.*]

> *A student writes 10 with lines:* | | | | | | | | | |

TEACHER: Another way?

> *A student writes with multiplication: 2 x 5*

TEACHER: How many numerals do we have in math? [*Lots of hands again.*]
STUDENTS: 10.
TEACHER: Why do you think we have 10 numerals?
STUDENTS: Because we have 10 fingers?
TEACHER: How many numbers can we make with that?
STUDENTS: Zillions.
TEACHER: What if we were aliens with only one finger on each hand? How many numerals might we have?

STUDENTS: Two.
TEACHER: How many numbers could we write out of two numerals?
STUDENTS: Not many.
TEACHER: And what would that do to our number system?
STUDENTS: There would be a problem.
TEACHER: What sort of problem?
STUDENTS: They couldn't do this.

> *Students hold up seven fingers.*

TEACHER: And why is that a problem?

Figure 3.2. Example of Socratic Method. From *The Socratic Method: Teaching by Asking Instead of Telling* by R. Garlikov, 2014, http://www.garlikov.com/Soc_Meth.html. Copyright 2014 by R. Garlikov. Reprinted with permission.

Grading a discussion can be a little challenging, but taking copious notes on how a student responds and his level of understanding, or even recording the discussion for you to go back to later are methods you can use to assess a discussion.

Pros

- Discussion allows students to feel as though they have some participation in the class. This participation can engage the students and get them interested in the topic.

- A discussion lets the teacher know instantly whether a student understands the content or not. If a discussion is not going to the level of depth the teacher would expect it to, maybe the class needs to review certain concepts or have steps introduced to them. Discussions also provide the opportunity to give feedback to the students.

- Discussions allow students to have dialogue with one another. Students bring a lot of their own knowledge and insights to a discussion. They can provide lessons for others that you were not able to as the teacher. It also allows students to arrive at these insights through the organic development of the discussion. There can be many "a-ha moments" for a student in a good class discussion.

- Class discussions can develop public speaking skills. You should be giving your students every opportunity possible to publically speak. The more they engage in this, the more comfortable with public speaking they will be.

Cons

- Sometimes student-led discussions can get so far off task that they are counterproductive to what you are trying to accomplish. There is a fine balance between giving the students some freedom and having little to no guidance.

- Students who do not like to talk in public can disappear into the background. It helps to have a system in place to prevent this from happening. Students who like to discuss and who always volunteer can end up monopolizing the discussion if the teacher allows them to. If you see this happening, develop a random method of calling on students.

- Discussions require some preparation from the teacher. Many times teachers think leading a discussion is just a "winging-it" activity, and some teachers who are naturally gifted at discussion can get away with this. However, it is better to have thought-out and prepared questions ahead of time that will lead the class to the insightful dialogue you wish to achieve. You might not use all these questions, but it is better to have them and not need them than to need them and not have them.

INTERVIEWS

Students often imagine teachers as being the expert in our given discipline. If you are a language arts teacher, you are expected to be able to spell every single word in the English language correctly or to have read every book in the library. If you are a math teacher, you should know how to solve any math problem or know all the mathematical principles that govern the disclipline.

We as teachers know the truth: There are those times when we simply do not know the answer or we are teaching a topic we are not comfortable with. When I was asked to teach science to fifth and sixth graders, I had not taken a science class for 15 years. I was certainly no expert. When a student asked me a question, I would say, "That's a good question, why don't you look that up?" It seemed to the students as though I wanted them to learn the answer for themselves and to empower them, but in reality, I just did not know the answer and did not want to let on to that fact. Having students interview an expert on a topic is always a good learning tool that takes students to a real-world connection. Not only that, unlike using a book or the Internet to find an answer, the students can ask exactly what it is they want to know and receive an instant answer. There is no inferring or reading between the lines. It is a direct way to get content and insight about a topic.

What It Looks Like

Interviews can be done in a couple of ways. One way is for the student herself to locate an expert in a topic she wants to know more about and conduct an individual interview. The interview is tailored to this student's needs and she gains valuable information from the source. For example, I had students research a career they were interested in pursuing. Part of the project called for research to find out the educational requirements of the job, the salary, the availability of such jobs, and other basic information the student would need to know in order to pursue that career. I also required an interview with someone who was in that specific field. Overwhelmingly, the students got so much more from the interviews than from hours and hours of research. The interview allowed the students the freedom to ask the questions the research would not answer. How much do the interviewees like their jobs? What are the drawbacks to working in their fields? What should someone going into those careers know first and foremost? Students conducted these interviews face-to-face, over the phone, and through e-mail. Students created the questions before conducting the interviews, but had to be comfortable enough with the questioning to let the conversation develop naturally. To help with this, students practiced their interviews with other classmates so that they became familiar with the questions and comfortable enough to go off script if necessary.

A second way to conduct an interview is for the teacher to bring in an expert or panel of experts for the students to question. There does need to be a format to this process. You do not want to just turn students loose to ask any questions that come to mind. Students might ask off-topic questions or even inappropriate ones, and time that could have been spent getting valuable insight from the speaker is wasted. The way I set it up in my classroom was for the students to think about questions prior to the person coming in. We would compile a list of questions for the speaker as a class. I would typically send this to the speaker ahead of time so he knew what he was getting into and to allow for any preparation that might be necessary. I either asked the questions or divided them up amongst the students to be asked. I did allow time for students' impromptu questions at the end, and because we had established the standard for questions beforehand, these were usually stronger and more on topic. An example of this was an immigration unit for which I would bring in speakers not native to the United States to share their experiences. I had speakers from Kenya, Iran, Russia, Brazil, the United Kingdom, and other foreign countries. We asked them about what their perspective of the United States was before coming here, what brought them here, and whether they found it easy or difficult to adjust to life in the United States. This provided a wonderful perspective to students that they would not have gotten from reading a book or researching on the Internet. It brought the real world to them. As the teacher, I could certainly have told them about other peoples' experiences as immigrants, but I have never experienced life as an immigrant myself. Bringing in an expert took the learning to a deeper, more meaningful level.

Pros

- Being able to conduct an interview is a 21st-century skill. Students' future jobs might require such a skill, and having it will be an advantage over those who have not experienced it.
- The student or class can receive instant feedback on a question from the interviewee. This allows for follow-up questions as well, raising the ceiling on content because the expert can tailor the answers to the audience and provide specific feedback.
- The learning is more meaningful because the expert can provide insight and details that cannot be provided in other media. The expert can usually add more depth to the topic based on the fact that he is an expert. Either through experience or knowledge, this person understands the topic in a way those asking the questions cannot.
- The ability to be able to create effective questions means the students have to understand the topic well enough to break it down. Also, being able to create higher level questions for the interview requires a higher level of thinking.

Cons

- The interviewee might give information that is not factual or that is biased in such a way as to affect the integrity of the interview. You want to be sure the person you are interviewing is indeed an expert and a good fit for your class. Do plenty of research before choosing and contacting an interviewee.
- Students need to ask good questions. If the student does not take the time to think about and craft his questions, the interview can produce very little

insight. In an interview, you get what you ask for, literally. If you ask lower level questions designed to elicit a one- or two-word response, that is what you will get in return. If you want detailed, insightful answers, the questions need to be detailed and insightful as well. This is something that needs to be deliberately taught to students rather than assuming it will happen on its own.

- Interviews do not necessarily stand on their own as assessments. Measuring what the student has learned can be a little tricky. How do the students display what they have learned? If they simply produce a transcript of the interview, it will not show specifically what they got out of it. You have to make sure you follow up with an additional assessment, such as a written reflection, to gain a glimpse into students' insights.

PORTFOLIOS

A student portfolio is a collection of materials that represents what a student learned. It may be something as simple as a folder containing the student's best work along with the student's evaluation of this work. It may also be articles or work from other sources that the student has commented or reflected on. The length of the portfolio is determined by the teacher. The portfolio could be a snapshot of what the student learned during a brief one-week project, or it can be an ongoing evolution of how that student has improved over the course of an entire year. For instance, the first part of a portfolio might contain an essay the student wrote on the first day of class. The remaining content of the portfolio might show work 6 weeks in, 12 weeks in, or at the semester break. What can be seen throughout this process is how the student has improved and acquired new skills or knowledge. Conceivably, a portfolio could track the student's progress for an entire year and even longer. The assessment of a portfolio comes more from the student commentary than it does from the pieces she selected as part of the portfolio. This commentary can be as informal as a student jotting down an observation from a highlighted piece of text to a formal essay that sums up the entire project or semester. Either one of these can be used in the classroom as a performance-based assessment.

What It Looks Like

According to Melissa Kelly (2014), there are three main factors that go into the development of a student portfolio assessment:

1. First, you must decide the purpose of your portfolio. For example, the portfolios might be used to show student growth, to identify weak spots in student work, and/or to evaluate your own teaching methods.

2. After deciding the purpose of the portfolio, you will need to determine how you are going to grade it. In other words, what would a student need in her portfolio for it to be considered a success and for her to earn a passing grade?

3. What should be included in the portfolio? Are you going to have students put of all their work or only certain assignments? Who gets to choose? (para. 9)

I taught science and did not use the long-term portfolios. My classroom portfolios charted the duration of a particular project and were used to indicate how the student went about learning the topic. I used two different formats for the portfolios. The first was a paper portfolio in which students placed found articles, textbook excerpts, or even pictures that provided them with information about a topic. Students would highlight, make notes in the margins, or add Post-it notes with their own commentary on what they got from a certain passage or visual. At the end of each article, the students would summarize what they learned and add any insights. I evaluated the students on whether they seemed to have an understanding of what they were commenting on. I was always looking for those unique insights students added to the material. For instance, if the students were doing a project on energy, there might be a series of pages the students printed out from the Internet, maybe photocopies of a chapter from the science book the students used, or perhaps an article from *Popular Mechanics* or *Newsweek* having to do with different types of energy. There should be a clear link between the contents and the learning objective the student is trying to demonstrate. If the learning objective has to do with energy conservation, the students might print a list they got from the Internet with tips on how energy can be conserved. The students might attach a Post-it note and comment, "I leave the television on all the time when I am out of the room. I will make sure to turn it off from now on." Then the students might summarize the article at the end like this:

> This website taught me about ways to conserve energy. One way is recycling. You can recycle by throwing your aluminum cans in the recycling bin. You can recycle and conserve energy in many ways, and I learned that from this website.

Another option I gave students was an electronic portfolio. An electronic portfolio provides links to websites the reviewer can click on. The students include these links and add their reflections and insights below the links. Figure 3.3 is what an electronic portfolio might look like. The important thing to keep in mind is to figure out what you want the portfolio to reflect about the learning and progression of the students and set it up accordingly.

ENERGY

Introduction

I have learned many things about energy and how it helps us in everyday life, such as powering our appliances or powering our cars. Here are a few websites that helped me. Also, I told why I liked these websites and what I learned from each of them.

- http://www.eia.doe.gov/kids/energyfacts/sources/whatsenergy.html
- http://www.eia.doe.gov/kids/energyfacts/science/formsofenergy.html

These websites are good websites because they helped me with many standards. One thing I learned is that there are two types of energy: kinetic (working energy) and stored (potential energy). Kinetic energy can be thermal, radiant, electrical, sound, and motion energy. Stored energy can be chemical, stored mechanical, nuclear, and gravitational energy types. These two websites helped me with learning the basics about energy.

Objective 1

Explain that the energy found in nonrenewable resources such as fossil fuels (e.g., oil, coal, and natural gas) originally came from the sun and may renew slowly over millions of years.

- http://www.energyquest.ca.gov/story/chapter08.html

This website was helpful because I learned that the energy fossil fuels use initially came from the sun and became stored energy by the photosynthesis in plants and small organisms. I also learned that when fossil fuels are being burned as a means of creating energy, they release harmful gases and pollutants in the air. This is how this website has helped me learn about fossil fuels.

- http://www.solcomhouse.com/fossilfuels.htm

I learned many things from this website about energy. From this website I learned that fossil fuels were formed from the sun's energy and during the Carboniferous period in time. I learned that the Carboniferous period was moist and warm, which is the kind of climate coal needs to form. I learned that it takes 210 years for coal to form. This is what the website taught me about when fossil fuels were formed.

Figure 3.3. Sample electronic portfolio.

Pros

- Portfolios help students who have difficulty seeing the big picture. Because a portfolio charts the progress of the project, it is constructed piece by piece. At the end, the students have an overall picture of how the pieces fit together. This helps them to see the project as a whole and to draw from it what they learned.
- Portfolios are good for helping students to develop a set of criteria. Because they are evaluating either their own work or that of a classmate, students must

come up with an evaluation system to do so. Evaluation is on the higher level of Bloom's (1956) taxonomy and thus employs higher level thinking skills.

- Students can get a good idea of how they learn. Because a portfolio tracks progress over a given period of time, the students can see strengths of what they did well and weaknesses of things that need to be worked on.

- Portfolios give the teacher a good idea of the thought processes of the students. Strengths and weaknesses in the way students gather information or approach a project can be seen. This allows the teacher to be able to make suggestions for how the students can learn better.

- There is a great deal of reflection in a portfolio, and students do not typically get enough opportunity to do this. Reflection is definitely thinking at a higher level, where one evaluates what was done well and what needs to be worked on. This is a skill few young people (and even adults) possess but one that makes people more self-aware. Self-awareness is a good quality to have because it allows one to build on strengths, avoid situations that would play into weaknesses, and become a stronger learner.

Cons

- Portfolios can be a lot of work, both for the students and the teacher. This requires from the teacher not just an understanding of the subject area the portfolio is covering, but what goes into a portfolio and the process used to develop it as well. Grading a portfolio can also be time consuming.

- If you are not keeping an eye on the progress of the student, a bad portfolio can be the result. Because students are not as familiar with using portfolios as a learning technique as others, the teacher must be purposeful about modeling what a good portfolio looks like and keeping track of student progress. With a classroom of 30 students, this can be a challenge but is worth the extra effort.

- The grading of a portfolio can be very subjective. The data tends to be qualitative rather than quantitative. There needs to be a clear criteria matched with a rubric that captures this criteria. If this is not clear, the results can be mixed.

EXHIBITIONS

An exhibition is just as it states: an exhibit of what the students have learned. The exhibition is usually viewed by an audience, whether it is made up of other students in the class, other classes from the school, parents, or outside audience members. The tricky thing about an exhibition is that the students cannot explain themselves orally; they must let the work explain itself. The analogy I often use with students when demonstrating an exhibition is the telling of a joke: "Two guys walk into a bar. The third one ducks." Nearly every time I tell this joke, I get puzzled looks and furrowed brows. I always feel a need to explain the joke: "You see, the bar in this case is not an establishment where one purchases alcohol. The bar is an actual metal bar that the people physically walk into . . ."

It's hilarious, right? Wrong. Because I have to explain the joke, it is not funny (no matter how much I think it is). Exhibitions are the exact same way. If you have to verbally explain the exhibit, the exhibit is not accomplishing what it is supposed to. When you go to an art exhibition, the artist is not there to explain what she did and why she did it. The piece has to stand on its own merits.

What It Looks Like

How a student approaches an exhibition is very different from other PBAs. Let us say for the sake of argument that a student creates a trifold as a product. If the student were using an oral presentation as this performance assessment, he might have a few meaningful visuals such as photos or graphs to enhance his explanation. He would not write out everything he plans to say on the board. Otherwise, he will feel compelled to read it verbatim and give a very stiff oral presentation. In an exhibition, the explanation would need to be written out because there is no one there to orally explain it. Figure 3.4 is an example of what a PowerPoint slide might look like for an exhibition. Notice how detailed it is. Even the visual has an explanation under it to provide helpful information to the viewers. By contrast, a slide for an oral presentation would contain the bare minimum: a title, the visual, and some sparse bullet points designed to remind the speaker of what he will be talking about in detail and to point out the most important take-aways to the audience. The presenter will explicate all of the details.

An exhibition can come in many forms. A few common ones include:

- a trifold,
- a poster,
- a PowerPoint presentation,
- a video,
- a piece of artwork or a craft, or
- a photography series.

No matter which form a student chooses, first and foremost it must inform the audience and allow it to learn from the exhibition.

Pros

- If there is a written aspect to the exhibition, it forces students to be detailed. Gifted students especially sometimes have difficulty going into detail. They

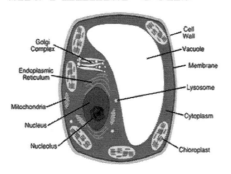

Differences Between Plant and Animal Cells

Golgi Complex
Endoplasmic Reticulum
Mitochondria
Nucleus
Nucleolus

Cell Wall
Vacuole
Membrane
Lysosome
Cytoplasm
Chloroplast

The picture above shows the structure of a plant cell. As you can see, a plant cell has a very distinct shape, compared to an animal cell, which is usually a random shape, considering the cells specialized job. The cell in the picture above has something called a cell wall. Which is the material on the outer most part of the cell. Animal cells don't consist of a cell wall.

There are multiple differences when it comes to plant and animal cells. Even though the 2 organisms both have cells, the cells in these organisms have many differences. One very obvious example of this is that plant cells, rather than animal cells have something called a cell wall. A cell wall is a structure around the outside of a plant cell. This specific structure is the reason why plant cells have such a distinct form. The cell wall is located around the outside of the cell membrane and protects the inside of the cell. It acts as a shield for the materials inside but also lets other supplies that are needed to enter. This is a difference between the animal cell and a plant cell because animals don't have a cell wall, they only have a cell membrane.

Figure 3.4. Sample PowerPoint slide.

assume everyone thinks the same way they do, and that a product does not need to be fully explained. An exhibition is designed to be shown to the public. If it is explained to students that the people viewing their exhibition will have no background knowledge and need everything explained, students might be motivated to make their products more detailed and informative.

- An exhibition is for all to see. Because of this, many will reap the benefits from what the exhibition has to teach, not just the one making it or grading it. Exhibitions allow others to experience what has been learned, and they can be inspirational for others. Rather than going through the hassle of taking the students to an expensive museum, you can have the students create the museum and learn from one another's exhibitions.

- They provide evidence of the kind of learning not typically reflected in objective multi-choice tests. Exhibitions can allow students to be creative. They can employ artistic skills that an essay or a multiple-choice assessment does not allow. Because this is a visual assessment, it opens itself up to all sorts of interesting ways to express oneself in this medium.

- They are great for connecting to the community. Inviting in community members to view exhibitions is a wonderful way to connect the two groups. Community members get to see what is being done in the school, and students can take the opportunity to receive feedback and explain face to face what they have learned.

Cons

- Sometimes students can get caught up in the production of the exhibition. If a student decides to draw a gorgeous pencil etching of the Eiffel Tower for her French class, the skill this reflects is simply of drawing. How is what has been learned in French class reflected in this exhibition other than the fact that the Eiffel Tower resides in that country? Is there a better way to reflect what has been learned about French culture? The teacher needs to be sure to keep the students focused on what they are trying to teach others with their exhibit.

- Because the exhibitions are for all to see, this leaves students open to criticism from many different sources. Some students are very uncomfortable with this. Some have a difficult time sharing their work with fellow students, much less outside people. You will have to make sure students are comfortable enough with this to be able to get their work done. Otherwise, a student might sabotage her own work just so she does not have to share it in a public forum.

- Your exhibitions are a reflection of you as a teacher. If you do not model for students what makes a good exhibition, the products you get could be hit or miss. And then not only is the work reflecting poorly on the student, it reflects poorly on you as the teacher as well. Exhibitions require you as the teacher to put yourself out there. Even when students have produced a good piece of work, if it is too controversial, it could reflect badly on you as the teacher to the community.

ESSAYS

Essays are often thought of only for use in language arts class, but essays can be used for any subject area concerning any topic. An essay basically asks a student to explain what she has learned in written form. You would think this would simply be a translation of what the student is thinking into words, but that is easier said than done. Many gifted students have difficulty making this translation, so is important to teach writing in all subject areas so that students become familiar with how to make this translation.

What It Looks Like

Essays have a basic five-part structure to them, which is shown in Figure 3.5. I like to use this visual with students because it makes the structure more concrete and sticks in students' minds.

I explain the purpose for each of these sections of the essay:

- Thesis Statement: This explains the purpose of the essay. It can be thought of as an introduction, but the thesis should be reiterated throughout the essay. This should be strong enough to be able to be backed up with three pieces of evidence.
- Evidence #1: This lays out the evidence that proves the thesis with supporting details. This might be an example from the text (language arts), an example problem (math or science), or a citation of a specific event that backs your thesis (social studies).
- Evidence #2: This is the same as evidence #1, but with a second example.
- Evidence #3: This is the same as evidence #1 and #2, but with a third example.
- Conclusion: This summarizes the main thesis and the arguments made. Lots of gifted students like to skip this step because they think they are just repeating themselves. Their rationale is, "What, is the person reading this dumb and need everything repeated?" My answer to them is that it is safest to assume nothing about the reader and be as clear as possible.

I establish this pattern with students at the very beginning of the year by having them write about their favorite color. Students must choose a favorite color (their thesis), give three reasons why it is their favorite color (evidence #1–#3), and make a final argument for the color (conclusion). I do this with third through twelfth grade. Many times we as teachers assume older students coming to us already know how to write an essay. Even in gifted education, reinforcement for valuable skills is always a good thing. Going over this simple structure can go a long way in providing you with clear essays.

Pros

- Students truly have to understand a topic in order to write an essay about it. A multiple-choice assessment allows students to either guess or memorize the information only long enough to take the assessment. An essay requires a little more enduring understanding. How can a student make an argument if he does not truly understand the topic?
- It is so much easier to ask a higher level question using an essay than it is in a multiple-choice assessment. Although higher level multiple-choice questions are possible, the nature of giving students choices makes it difficult to reach a higher level of thinking. Essays, on the other hand, provide a lot of openness

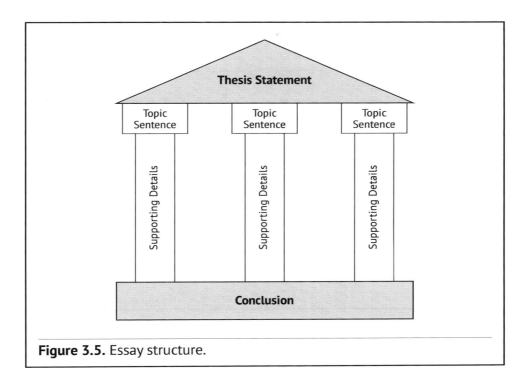

Figure 3.5. Essay structure.

for students to explore topics and access their higher level thinking skills. The teacher still has to write good essay questions that allow students to do this and to explore and make arguments.

- Students have to express their thoughts in written form. This is a valuable 21st-century skill to learn. Strong writers are more rare than one would think. According to a study published in *The Chronicle of Higher Education*, only 6% of college professors view their students as well-prepared writers (Sanoff, 2006). Forty-four percent even say that their students are not ready for college-level writing (Sanoff, 2006). Having a student who is a strong writer will provide an advantage for her, distinguishing her from other students and/or workers.

- Essays allow students to be creative. If they use an analogy to make a point or compare it, students will tap into their own experiences. It allows them to make a connection to something real. It also allows the student to look at an assignment from another perspective. If a student were asked to describe a submarine, the normal answer might describe the steel hull, the propeller, and the periscope that allows them to see above the surface of the water. Another student might describe it as having two pieces of bread with various meats, vegetables, and maybe a slice of cheese in between. Neither student is incorrect. Each is just looking at the question differently. Essays allow for different and unique perspectives to emerge.

Cons

- Essays certainly take longer to grade. There have been many times I have been hunkered down at my desk for a 3-hour grading session with a stack of essays by my side and I have said to myself, "Just once couldn't you give them a multiple-choice assessment and give yourself a break?" But after reading all of my students' essays, it is very clear that they are learning more this way. Not only that, they are learning at a higher level of thinking. They have to analyze a question and figure out how they are going to answer it, synthesize the information they have learned, discern what would and would not be good to use, and evaluate the evidence they are using to determine if their response is convincing or not. It is a trade-off. You will spend more time grading essays, but by employing them, you know your students are learning more.

- Grading essays can be interpreted as subjective. In other words, if three different teachers grade an essay, would they all three give the exact same grade? Probably not. A student's grade might be subject to the whim of a teacher. Maybe one teacher values something more than another. The way around this, of course, is to have a proper rubric to make the grading as objective as possible. As the teacher, you would want to share this rubric with the students so they are aware of how the essay was evaluated and they can see why they got the grade they did.

- An essay exam cannot cover as much material as a multiple-choice assessment. You could ask 30 multiple-choice questions that cover a variety of topics in the time it may take a student to answer one essay question. Although you certainly have more depth in an essay, you do not have as much breadth. Depending on the topic you are teaching, breadth might be necessary. If students are learning their multiplication tables, breadth is going to be more important than writing an essay about why knowing the multiplication tables is valuable.

RESEARCH PAPERS

One way to look at a research paper is as an expanded essay. Essentially, it follows the same structure: introduction of thesis, evidence, and conclusion. The big difference is that students are also responsible for conducting independent research. In an essay, the teacher provides the background information or data for a student to be able to answer the question presented in an essay format. The students are merely synthesizing what they have learned from the teacher and communicating how it fits into the essay. The essay can be written on the spot and is a culmination of what has been taught. A research paper, on the other hand, has the students acquiring the information for themselves by using various sources including books, the Internet, or interviews. The writing aspect is the last thing the student will be doing. There is the process of finding, evaluating, and organizing the information. Finally, the student must properly cite this information and its sources.

What It Looks Like

The key to a good research paper is providing an outline for students to follow. The outline can be very basic or it can be detailed depending on the level of the student. The outline should walk students step by step through what is expected in the paper. Students should be able to use this as a blueprint to construct their research paper.

It is important for students to understand there is a structure to a research paper and that the outline is the backbone upon which they will build the research around. Once they understand this and have a solid outline, the creation of the paper becomes a matter of building it around the outline. This will make the writing of all future research papers easier.

Pros

- Research papers are not reports or a regurgitation of information. A research paper is an interpretation and evaluation of information as well as a display of higher level critical-thinking skills. Students receive the benefits both of writing the paper and conducting the research. Students are gaining two 21st-century skills for the price of one assessment.
- Students will be expected to write research papers when they get to college or even at their jobs. Students who are able to write good research papers have an advantage over those who do not. Depending on the style of the documentation, students will be learning technical writing. This can be a beneficial style to learn for those seeking 21st-century careers.
- Research papers make it easy to evaluate multiple disciplines across the curriculum. For instance, if students are writing a research paper about mathematics in nature using the Fibonacci Sequence as the guiding topic, the math teacher can grade the paper looking at the mathematical terms involved, the science teacher can evaluate the paper and the interactions in nature, and the language arts teacher can look at the paper to determine whether the student used proper sentence structure, grammar, spelling, etc. One assessment can be evaluated by multiple subject areas focusing on different skills.
- Research papers are not just about the writing. Students are also learning the skill of research. We already discussed that conducting research comprises informational literacy, which is a valuable 21st-century skill. In addition, there are several other benefits to conducting research (Lopatto, 2003):

▷ learning a topic in depth,

▷ the ability to work and think independently,

▷ the ability to read literature,

▷ improving oral and written communication,

▷ improving problem-solving skills,

▷ learning to appreciate a new subject,

▷ the practical application of course work,

▷ the enhancement of credentials,

▷ understanding the research process, and

▷ learning to work independently.

■ Research papers are good to use as a culminating experience. They can help assess students' overall ability in your classroom. Some schools use a senior thesis, universities use dissertations, but the same idea is that the students are summing up their learning experiences through the use of a research paper. You will be able to see if students truly understand the content. Students can use the lower level thinking skill of memorization for an exam, but to be able to communicate a topic in written form, students need to be able to fully understand it.

Cons

■ Research papers can be time consuming to grade. If you have 25 students in a class, each writing a five-page research paper, you will be reading 125 pages of student work. However, as with other time-consuming PBAs, I have found the benefits far outweigh the inconveniences.

■ Research papers take a long time to teach and write. You would not be able to assign a research paper to be done in just a week's time. It might take a month for the students to conduct the research and write the paper, perhaps longer. This is a long time to devote to one given project in a classroom.

■ Research papers open up the very ugly problem of plagiarism. It is a rampant form of cheating. There are students who will cut and paste entire passages or not cite a source simply because it is easier not to do so. The consequences of such an act need to be clear to students, and when a student does it, it needs to be handled as a disciplinary measure on the same level as any other form of cheating. You have to be sure to teach students what it means to plagiarize, how to correctly put things into their own words, and how to properly document sources. You want students to learn this lesson now when the only thing at stake is their grade; if caught cheating in college or in the workplace, they could get expelled or fired.

JOURNALS/STUDENT LOGS

Journals and student logs allow for a more informal style of writing. Although it is important for students to be able to write a proper essay, it is also important to give students the opportunity to be creative and not be constrained by the structure of an essay. Journals and student logs allow students to explore ideas without being tied to an essay format. The format need not even include complete sentences. Students could draw, write poetry, make lists, write letters from the perspective of another person, draw charts, or use any other form of expression.

Journals also do not need to be exclusive to language arts class. Students can journal in science, social studies, math, even gym classes. The nice thing about using journals is that they show the progression of learning. Students can go back and see how much they have learned and what route they took to get there.

What It Looks Like

The nice thing about journal entries is that unlike an essay or research paper, which has a clear structure, there is more flexibility to look like whatever the teacher or student wishes for it to be. Journal entries usually start with a prompt. Writing prompts using higher level language allows for higher level thinking. It is important not to encourage lower level journal entries by assigning lower level prompts. Using key words from Bloom's taxonomy to do this will help in the writing of these higher level prompts (Sedita, 2012).

Instead of using prompts that begin with the ones in Figure 3.6, try prompts that begin with the higher level words in Figure 3.7. This allows students to create at a higher level and taps into their gifted potential and creativity.

Pros

- Journals allow students the opportunity to reflect. Assessments often simply determine whether a student knew the content or not. Rarely are students afforded the chance to reflect upon what worked in a project and what did not. When students have time to assess their efforts and experiences for a given project, they can figure what sort of learners they are and what works best for their style of learning. It is so important to figure this out so they can play to their strengths and limit the amount of exposure to those skills they are not as strong in. This awareness is an important trait as a student and lifelong learner.
- Journals allow students to be creative. We do a lot of technical writing in school, but how much opportunity is given to students to be creative and have fun with writing? Students need to know that writing can be a joy and

Remembering	Where is . . . What did . . . Who was . . . When did . . . How many . . . Locate in the story . . . Point to the . . .
Understanding	Tell me in your own words . . . What does it mean . . . Give me an example of . . . Describe what . . . Make a map of . . . What is the main idea of . . .
Applying	What would happen to you if . . . Would you have done the same as . . . If you were there, would you . . . How would you solve the problem . . . In the library, find information about . . .

Figure 3.6. Lower level prompts.

not something to dread. If a teacher were to simply assign an essay on how Atticus Finch felt in defending Tom Robinson in *To Kill a Mockingbird*, the students might find this a very workmanlike task. However, if the teacher instead asked the students to write a diary entry from the perspective of Atticus Finch, it allows the students to be much more creative and to tap into what it might have been like to be Atticus. This is going to allow the student to have empathy for the character and understand his perspective a little better.

- When students are journaling during the process of learning, teachers will get to see students' mistakes and successes. When students turn in final papers or assignments, we often hope that they are devoid of mistakes. The students (we hope) have edited those out so the teacher is presented only with the correct information. Seeing mistakes, however, can be valuable for both the teacher and the student. The teacher sees how a student overcame an obstacle, what he decided to do as an alternative, and whether the student avoided other mistakes. When it comes to learning, seeing how students learn from these mistakes will provide teachers with much insight about what kind of learners the students are.

Analyzing	What things would you have used . . . What other ways could . . . What things are similar/different? What things couldn't have happened in real life? What kind of person is . . . What caused _____ to act the way she/he did?
Evaluating	Would you recommend this book? Why? Why not? Select the best . . . Why is it the best? What do you think will happen to . . . Why do you think that? Rank the events in order of importance. Which character would you most like to meet? Why? Was _____ good or bad? Why? Did you like the story? Why?
Creating	What would it be like if . . . What would it be like to live . . . Design a . . . Pretend you are a . . . What would have happened if . . . Why/why not? Use your imagination to draw a picture of . . . Add a new item on your own . . . Tell/write a different ending . . .

Figure 3.7. Higher level prompts.

Cons

- With the expression of emotions can sometimes come some dark feelings from students. These thoughts can be about wanting to hurt oneself, being hurt by others, or emotions that students are having a difficult time understanding. As teachers, this can be uncomfortable to deal with. We are not necessarily trained to deal with such problems, but we are also aware that we care about these kids. When you run across something that is suspicious, it is important to notify the proper people that can help with the situation, whether it is the school social worker, psychologist, or counselor. The bad news is that you might be put in an uncomfortable position for a little while. The good news is that it will allow you to help a student get out of his or her uncomfortable place.
- You have to be willing to carve out the time for students to write in their student journals/logs. Because the style is more informal, you are not grading these according to grammar, spelling, structure, etc. You are simply allowing students a chance to explore their feelings and possibly vent through writing.

Some teachers in today's day and age of Common Core standards feel the pressure of not having enough time to get in everything that needs to be covered. There is some hesitation to devote class time for students to explore their feelings, but doing so will create more self-reflective learners.

- Because journals do not have a strong structure, you are going to get unstructured entries. Although this allows for much creativity, it can also allow for much chaos on the page. Some students do not know how to communicate without some kind of structure in place. No matter what method the students use, they still have to be able to communicate an idea through the journal entry. This can be a hard lesson for some.

SUMMARY

There are many other possibilities for PBAs than the 10 discussed here. I have seen teachers use lessons from the Royal Shakespeare Company to analyze and take apart text using performance activities to amazing results. I have seen students make films that encapsulate a historical event or recreate a scene from a book. I have had students draw comic books that demonstrate scientific law through the powers of a superhero. With a PBA, the sky is the limit. However, if you are just being introduced to the practice, it is important to start with something simple. One thing that can get teachers trying to use performance-based assessment into trouble is when they bite off more than they can chew. Just like a student learning math, you cannot just jump into complex algebraic equations. There are many simple concepts the student needs to understand first before he can be successful. The same goes for PBA—try some of these suggestions to gain a basic understanding of PBA before moving onto more complicated tasks and activities.

CHAPTER 4

How To Teach Performance-Based Assessment

Teaching performance-based assessment to students can be a challenge, especially if they have never encountered it before. Anything new can seem uncomfortable to a student, but remember, it is in this state of risk when the greatest learning takes place.

If students are too comfortable, little learning takes place. On the other end of the spectrum, when students feel too much discomfort, they are unable to focus on learning. Performance-based assessment has to carefully walk the tightrope of risk to ensure the most learning is going to take place.

How do you walk that tightrope? How do you make students familiar enough with PBA that they do not feel that they are in the "danger zone"? You as the teacher can greatly influence performance-based assessment in a positive manner. Here are some tips on how to do that:

1. Select assessment tasks that are clearly aligned or connected to what has been taught.
2. Share the scoring criteria for the assessment task with students prior to working on the task.
3. Provide students with clear statements of standards and/or several models of acceptable performances before they attempt a task.
4. Encourage students to complete self-assessments of their performances.
5. Interpret students' performances by comparing them to standards that are developmentally appropriate, as well as to other students' performances (Baker, O'Neill, & Linn, 1993, pp. 1210–1218).

The first step is selecting assessment tasks that are clearly aligned or connected to what has been taught. This can be accomplished by defining the criteria for what is expected in the performance-based assessment.

DEFINING THE CRITERIA

It is necessary that you make it perfectly clear to students what the learning objectives for the PBA are. This should be transparent to students so that at any given time, they are aware of what it is they are supposed to be learning. When students lose sight of this, they get into trouble and their work suffers. That is why clear criteria are so important.

When creating your learning objectives, Herman, Aschbacher, and Winters (1992) suggest that educators ask themselves five questions:

1. What important cognitive skills or attributes do I want my students to develop (e.g., to communicate effectively in writing, to analyze issues using primary source and reference materials, to use algebra to solve everyday problems, etc.)?

2. What social and affective skills or attributes do I want my students to develop (e.g., to work independently, to work cooperatively with others, to have confidence in their abilities, to be conscientious, etc.)?

3. What metacognitive skills do I want my students to develop (e.g., to reflect on the writing processes they use; to evaluate the effectiveness of their research strategies, to review their progress over time, etc.)?

4. What types of problems do I want them to be able to solve (e.g., to undertake research, to understand the types of practical problems that geometry will help them solve, to solve problems that have no single correct answer, etc.)?

5. What concepts and principles do I want my students to be able to apply (e.g., to understand cause-and-effect relationships, to apply principles of ecology and conservation in everyday lives, etc.)? (pp. 25–26)

Many times these criteria can be linked to Common Core standards or 21st-century skills. Once you have established these criteria, it is important to communicate them to students as well as parents and any other pertinent stakeholders. This can come in a number of different ways, including:

- a syllabus,
- a contract, or
- a rubric.

A syllabus is simply an explanation of what is it you hope to accomplish as a teacher in this performance-based assessment. This is explained to students at the very beginning of the process. This way, every action they take leads them toward this outcome/assessment. There should be no hidden agendas or skills you are evaluating that were not made clear at the beginning of the unit. Figure 4.1 is an example of a syllabus.

This method leaves the teacher as the sole decision maker, however. If you want a method that has more student input, it's best to use a contract. A contract is usually created collaboratively by the teacher and the students. The teacher might have certain skills and standards she would like the students to use, while the students might have certain skills they feel they are strong in or would like to include in the PBA. Figure 4.2 is an example of what a contract might look like.

The final way to establish the criteria is through the use of a rubric. A rubric can be created by the teacher, the students, or both. This process will be discussed further in Chapter 5. A rubric might look like the one shown in Figure 4.3.

Any of these methods gives students a clear picture of what they need to do to create an excellent performance assessment. The most important thing is that students get these criteria *prior* to working on the performance assessment. The criteria are like a blueprint; without them, the students will not know how to build a strong PBA.

MODELING

As much as knowing the criteria ahead of time is valuable, actually being able to model what a PBA looks like is important for student understanding. This is especially helpful to those students who are kinesthetic or visual learners and have trouble seeing the big picture in abstract terms.

It is important to allow students to try a PBA first in a situation where there are no consequences. This allows those kinesthetic and visual learners to actually get to play with the assessment a little bit to try to gain a full understanding of what can be done.

For example, let us say you ask students to engage in a debate using the specific Lincoln-Douglas format as a PBA. You want students to experience the format first so you set up mini-debates at the beginning of the unit where students can get a feel for what the Lincoln-Douglas structure is really like. These mini-debates do not need to be complicated or require research; they can be over simple topics just so students can get used to the format. Below are some sample mini-debate topics:

- Practice Debate #1: The chicken should cross the road.
- Practice Debate #2: Math is a useless subject.
- Practice Debate #3: Students should be allowed to chew gum in school.

The three topics are fairly easy to debate. Students typically have no problem diving into them and creating an organized debate. No one is being graded here, but an evaluation should take place after each practice debate. Have the students reflect

---

WORLD RELIGIONS PROJECT SYLLABUS

Learning Goals
1. To increase student knowledge and understanding of the major world religions.
2. To see how the religion has spread throughout many countries.
3. To compare and contrast religions with one another.
4. To teach others about the religion as well as learn from others.
5. To have interaction with someone from the religion.

Standard
  Modern cultural practices and products show the influence of tradition and diffusion, including the impact of major world religions (Buddhism, Christianity, Hinduism, Islam, Taoism, Sikhism, and Judaism).

21st-Century Skills
- Research
- Interview
- PowerPoint
- Presentations
- Collaborative group work

Performance Assessment
  PowerPoint Presentation that will include:
1. Section A: Give the basic beliefs and traditions of the religion including:
   - Geographic origins
   - Founding leaders
   - Teachings

2. Section B: Use maps to show the origins and spread of your religion including the major countries that currently worship it.
3. Section C: Interview someone who practices the religion you are studying. Through these interviews students will gain different perspectives for how the religion is viewed and worshipped. As a group, students will present a written list of the essential questions and answers from the interview, as well as an analysis of what they learned. Interviews can be done:
   - Face to face
   - Phone
   - Internet/Skype

Figure 4.1. Sample syllabus.

on what worked well or how the arguments could have been strengthened. This act of modeling will get the students more familiar not only with the format, but with what an excellent PBA looks like. You want to make sure students have a basic understanding of how to create the PBA they are being expected to carry out. Modeling is an excellent way to do that.

PROJECT CONTRACT

Project Topic: World Religions

Essential Question: Show the influence of tradition and diffusion, including the impact of major world religions.

Learning Outcomes:
1. To increase knowledge and understanding of the major world religions.
2. To see how the religion has spread throughout many countries.
3. To have interactions with someone who practices that religion.

Product of Project: A mock news program where each segment will show the aspects of a religion and its influence. The program should include one of the following:
- A news anchor who will provide an overview of the religion and its basic tenets.
- An on-the-spot reporter who will be at a few events that show the influence of the religion.
- A "weather man" who will use maps to show how the religion has spread.
- An interview with the person who practices that religion.

Figure 4.2. Sample project contract.

USE OF PAST EXAMPLES

You do not always know what you will get when you conduct performance-based assessments for the very first time. You can set criteria and model what the expectations will be, but sometimes students will go above and beyond what you expected—and at other times, you might get something you are just not pleased with.

For example, I did a PBA with students concerning the expansion of the United States. One group of students chose the steamboat as their topic, and their essential question was "How did the invention and use of the steamboat allow the United States to expand as a nation?" This was the first time I had done such a project with the students, and although I set up clear criteria, I did not do a good job of modeling what I wanted the PBA to look like. I thought this might influence what I got from the students and wanted to see what they could come up with on their own. The steamboat group spent a lot of time in the back workroom. Every time I checked in with them, they seemed to be working well together and appeared to have a clear plan for how they were going to teach the class about the influence of the steamboat. When they gave their presentation, there was a lot of style to the content, but very little substance. The focal point of their presentation was a paper steamboat that took them hours to construct but that did not teach anything to the class. Unfortunately, at the end of their performance assessment, the other students did not have a clue about how the steamboat helped with the expansion of the United States. I did not even have to tell the group that their lesson was not very strong—they sensed it from the audience reaction and upon hearing themselves give the lesson out loud. We had

WORLD RELIGIONS PRESENTATION

Students: _____   Religion: _____

Overall	Content	Presentation	Maps
Excellent (A)	▪ Includes many details and examples designed to back up what the student is saying. ▪ Research is from reliable sources. ▪ Interview adds much to the presentation, giving perspective to the religion.	▪ PowerPoint has a flow to it ▪ PowerPoint uses meaningful visuals that add to the content of the presentation. ▪ Speakers present clearly and do not read the PowerPoint to audience.	▪ Includes five maps that show the clear progress of the spread of the religion. ▪ Includes a map/chart indicating where the religion is practiced widely today, including statistics or percentages of followers.
Good (B-C)	▪ Has a few details and examples to back up points but could use more. ▪ Most of the research is from reliable sources but some is questionable or not correct. ▪ Interview is included and gives some information on the religion but does not add anything to the content.	▪ PowerPoint jumps around some, making it hard to follow at times. ▪ PowerPoint uses visuals, but not all of them are meaningful. ▪ Speakers present clearly most of the time, but occasionally they read the presentation to the class.	▪ Includes three to four maps that show where the religion spread but not how. ▪ Includes map/charts showing places where the religion is practiced widely today but does not include numbers to back it up.
Needs Improvement (D-F)	▪ Does not use details and examples to back up points. ▪ Much of the research comes from questionable sources or is incorrect. ▪ Interview is not included or presents only a stereotype of the religion.	▪ PowerPoint is so unorganized it is difficult to figure out what is being presented. ▪ PowerPoint lacks visuals, or most of them add nothing to the content. ▪ Speakers read the entire presentation or do not make themselves clearly heard.	▪ Includes two or fewer maps that show the clear progress of the spread of the religion. ▪ Does not include map/chart indicating where the religion is practiced widely today.

Figure 4.3. Sample rubric.

a conference afterward during which we talked about what went wrong and where the missteps might have taken place. I asked them if I could keep their paper steamboat to use as an example of what not to do and the group unanimously agreed to let me. For the remainder of the year, whenever we would start another performance-based assessment, I would pull out the boat and say to the class, "Do not be the steamboat group." This made the class giggle and chuckle, even the steamboat group itself, but it also served as a reminder to avoid style over substance. They had all seen what had gone wrong and why it had not worked. I believe this example allowed me to prevent other groups from making the same mistake.

As a teacher, it would behoove you to collect samples of as many performance-based assessments as possible, and not only the good examples, but ones that were subpar as well. These examples can go a long way in allowing students to see what to do and what not to do. I would present these examples to the students and have them rate them using the rubric. It is always interesting to see that students, gifted students especially, are pretty tough graders. They expect a lot from a project when they are looking at someone else's work. But they are not always as skilled at scrutinizing their own work. By looking at someone else's PBA, they can see what makes an excellent assessment, but more importantly, what makes a poor one. Seeing the poor PBA prevents them from doing the same. No one wants to be the steamboat group.

I also would use student examples at the completion of a performance-based assessment so that students understood how they were graded and what they could improve on for next time. If students had written an essay, I would make overhead projections of poor, good, and excellent essays. I did not use any names, but I had the class read the essays and evaluate which ones are the poor, the good, and the excellent ones. Students can figure these out fairly quickly. We then discussed why each of the essays' quality fell where it does and what could have been done to improve it. This did a couple of things: It allowed me to review with any students who did not understand the concept the essay was supposed to explain, and it allowed students to see what the teacher's expectations were. This allowed them to be fully prepared the next time we did a similar PBA.

SHOWING STUDENTS REAL-WORLD EXAMPLES

In addition to showing the class past student examples, any time you can show real-world examples of performance-based assessments adds a whole different level to the understanding. One way to bring real-world connections into the classroom is by having students watch professionals doing their jobs. The Internet can be a great help in this. For example, if the students are to conduct an interview, have the class watch video clips from landmark interviews, such as David Frost interviewing Richard

Nixon. As a class, you can talk about what allowed the interview to be successful. If you are trying to see examples of good speeches, you could watch FDR's "Only Thing We Have to Fear Is Fear Itself" speech or Martin Luther King Jr.'s "I Have a Dream" speech. As a class, you could use the rubric on speeches to analyze what elements were successful. When it comes to exhibitions, you could look at real museum exhibits to see what makes an exhibit stand out and how well it communicates its information. You will want to have a class discussion on what makes a successful exhibition and how can the students replicate this in their own PBAs.

Another opportunity for real-world connections is having a professional come in and explain how he has to write research papers for his job or must give a presentation to his boss when he pitches a new project. Helping students to see how these performance based-assessments are used in the real world will only emphasize their importance and relevance. The parents of your students are always a good resource. Shoot an e-mail out to parents and see who does a particular PBA in their line of work and invite them to come speak to the class. It is a win-win because the students are getting to see the PBA used in the real world, and a member of the community is getting to share with the class.

STRESSING THE IMPORTANCE OF PRACTICE

Because this is a performance, students need to make sure to practice. If students are giving a performance for the very first time when they are being assessed on it, it is bound to be rife with mistakes that will only hurt their grades. When someone is putting on a play, the actors do not come together for the first time and give the performance on the spot. They rehearse their performance so that by the time the audience sees it, any wrinkles have been ironed out and the performers have confidence. I can always tell when students have or have not practiced their performance because it becomes painfully obvious. I always liken a performance to drafts of a paper. When students turn in a paper, they shouldn't turn in the first draft because it will be full of grammatical mistakes, incomplete thoughts, or other such errors that are usually found in first drafts. The students might go through two, three, maybe even four drafts, each one getting better because of the changes they make and problems they fix. The same goes for a performance. If students practice, they will become more confident, which will eliminate the distracting "ummms," "likes," and "yeahs" from a presentation. Students also might not find mistakes until they speak the words out loud. By practicing, these mistakes can be fixed before students get evaluated.

There are a few ways you can encourage your students to practice. First, you can devote some class time to practicing. Take a half hour or more to pair students off and practice the performance. Classmates can offer feedback to help the performance get better. When I had students presenting their Invention Convention in science,

I would spend an entire class having them go through their presentation numerous times, gaining confidence and picking up new suggestions each time they presented to another classmate.

A second method is to make parents or other teachers aware of the upcoming performance and ask them to act as an audience for the students. I actually made it a requirement for my science class for students to get a second evaluation of their performance assessment. I gave them a variety of choices for potential evaluators:

- another teacher,
- student peer,
- panel,
- parent/relative,
- mentor, or
- expert.

As part of their evaluations, students had to turn in a completed rubric from the person who had seen the practice performance. Another set of eyes is always going to be beneficial.

A third way to practice is to have students videotape and then watch themselves with the rubric in front of them. Students often catch things they were not even initially aware of. This allows them to not make the same mistake when it comes time to give the final performance. This self-evaluation of their work also allows the student to be reflective of the performance.

If you as the teacher do not model this idea of practicing a performance to the students, they will not likely take the initiative to do it on their own. You have to explain to them the importance of practicing and show them the benefits of doing it.

GIVING STUDENTS SPACE

One important but difficult element of teaching PBA is to give students space. This means providing students with a place and the resources to work on their PBAs. Students could practice in the hallway, in an empty classroom, in the gym while it's empty, or any other space you can get your hands on. Students need to be able to spread out and explore their thoughts and ideas. If students are performing a Shakespeare scene from a play they are working on, you want to be able to allow them to have a stage to do so. It might not be an actual stage, but after all, a stage is merely an open space. If students need to spray paint a product they are working on, allow them to go outside to do so but still be under the supervision of an adult. If they are filming, have a couple of classroom flip cameras, or if the budget does not allow for this, send a plea home asking for parents to send theirs in for students to borrow. If they need tools in order to construct a product, be willing to bring them in. Students will have difficulty getting a saw or hammer on the bus, so provide those tools for them if possible. Some teachers might not feel comfortable and just have those students work on those products at home, but then they'd miss the process of the construction of their PBAs. That is just as important as the final product. You want to see that student working away on his product or painting her mural with your own eyes. You just have to be cognizant of making sure the environment is safe for all students, and you do want to be courteous to your neighbors. You do not want your students yelling in the hallway and disturbing a nearby classroom. In my own experience, I once had students build catapults. I brought in the necessary tools and students were cutting, twisting, bending, and hammering their catapults. Then my phone rang. I answered it expecting to send a student out for early dismissal when my principal's voice came over the speaker.

"What on Earth are you doing up there?" she asked. "It sounds like the ceiling is coming down on me."

I had a second-floor classroom and her office was directly under us. All that banging was twice as loud for her. Once I explained what we were doing, I invited her up to come see the students in action. When she entered my classroom, she took one look at them and said,

"You guys just keep on working. I will just go on a stroll until you are finished."

She could see that students were engaged and learning. What principal would not want that? However, some administrators are a little less noise-tolerant, so be sure to seek out permission before taking on any noise-inducing activities.

It is also important to provide students with the mental space to work. Students tend to be a bit inhibited when an instructor is constantly scrutinizing. As the teacher, you are trying to help and monitor progress, but some students find this stifling to their creativity. You need to be able to back off and allow students the freedom to do their own thing. This seems daunting to some teachers, but if you have laid out the structure and expectations, students will be fine. You do want to schedule meetings with them from time to time, however, just to make sure they are on the right track. Otherwise, observe from afar unless you have students who ask for your help.

SUMMARY

The most important thing about PBA is clear communication. You should make sure you clearly communicate what you want to accomplish with a PBA so that students keep that at the forefront of their decisions as they align their PBAs to the learning objectives.

You also need to communicate the expectations of the project. This can be done in a number of ways but syllabi, contracts, or rubrics are a good means because not only do they inform the students, but parents can be made aware of what is expected as well. Communicating to students what a good assessment looks like through modeling can go a long way. When students get to experience the PBA, they gain a better understanding of it. Communicating what you expect when it comes to the quality of the work is essential. This can be done by showing them examples of excellent assessments and not-so-excellent ones and by linking them to real-world examples.

The final strategy that will help to teach your students the importance of PBA is encouraging students to practice. When this is communicated to students, they will give the final assessment more weight. Be sure you do not overcommunicate, though, and provide students the space to be able to complete their PBAs without you getting in the way of their creativity.

CHAPTER 5

How to Evaluate Performance-Based Assessments With Rubrics

One of the most attractive aspects of objective multiple-choice assessments is that they are quite easy to evaluate. You simply determine whether the student bubbled in the appropriate letter and if he did not, you mark it wrong. What could be more objective than that? Bias is usually not a factor because the answer is either right or wrong. There is none of that grayness we encounter as teachers when we have to interpret an essay or evaluate whether a presentation displayed the learning objectives or not.

Performance-based assessments are a little more challenging because they are not as black and white. There is a certain level of subjectivity when it comes to grading a PBA because you are judging a performance. The key is to minimize this subjectivity by making the grading criteria as clear as possible. This makes for a more successful evaluation of the PBA. One of the best ways to do this is through the creation of rubrics.

THE USE OF RUBRICS

The definition of a rubric provided by Judith Arter and Jay McTighe (2001) in their book *Scoring Rubrics in the Classroom: Using Performance Criteria for Assessing and Improving Student Performance* is "a particular format for criteria—it is the written-down version of the criteria, with all score points described and defined" (p. 8). They go on to further describe the qualities of a good rubric:

> The best rubrics are worded in a way that covers the essence of what we, as teachers, look for when we're judging quality, and they reflect the best thinking in the field as to what constitutes good performance. Rubrics are frequently accompanied by examples (anchors) of products or performances to illustrate the various score points on the scale. (p. 8)

There are many benefits to using rubrics, but for our purposes, we will focus on three of them. The first is that a rubric allows for consistency in scoring. This helps to solve some of the problem of subjectivity. A well-written rubric that clearly defines the criteria makes it easier for a teacher to be objective in the way she scores a student. Conversely, a poorly written rubric allows for much subjectivity. This is why it is so important to start with a well-written, well-structured rubric.

The second benefit of a well-written rubric is that it clarifies for students the expectations of the assessment and acts as a road map for them. If they follow this map, it guarantees them a good grade. It's when they do not follow the road map that they get lost and end up losing points as a result. Because of this, it is always a good idea to give students the rubric for the PBA at the very beginning of the unit. This should inform all of the students' decisions. If students are using a rubric correctly, they would have it out while they create their PBAs, making sure they are following the expectations laid out for an excellent result. Students should not be seeing a rubric for the first time when they receive their evaluations back. They should be aware of the expectations from the very beginning.

The third benefit of using rubrics is that they clarify the expectations for the teachers themselves. You would think this would be a given for educators, but sometimes teachers are not sure what to expect. When this happens, you get a mixed bag of results because students are not quite sure where to go because the teachers are not quite sure where to lead them. Creating rubrics clarifies for you, the teacher, what it is you hope students achieve on their assessments.

BUILDING YOUR RUBRICS

Once you have decided to use rubrics, the question becomes: Which type of rubric is best? There are three different decisions you need to make about your rubrics according to Arter and Jay McTighe (2001) in their book *Scoring Rubrics in the Classroom: Using Performance Criteria for Assessing and Improving Student Performance*:

- Are you measuring a holistic or analytical trait?

- Are you asking students to measure a general or a task-specific skill?
- Are you evaluating using points or letter grades? (p. 17)

A holistic rubric looks at a performance as a whole to give the teacher an over-all picture of what a student learned. The entire assessment is given a single grade depending on where on the rubric it lands. Figure 5.1 is what a holistic rubric used for an essay might look like. After the essay is read, the teacher should choose the rubric description that best fits it. The rubric does not include anything about spelling, structure, or organization. That means as long as the student covers the content indicated in the rubric, she will receive the grade that the rubric describes. The teacher cannot take off for something not included in the rubric.

An analytical trait rubric divides the assessment into traits. As a result, it breaks down the evaluation of the PBA for the student and each trait has its own grade. Figure 5.2 is what an analytical trait rubric might look like. Each of the traits—compare/contrast, theme, student reaction, and mechanics—are all given their own evaluation. The analytical rubric allows you to analyze each of the traits to be able to evaluate students with more specificity. You would be able to evaluate not only the content of the report, but the mechanics as well.

The second decision you need to make is whether the rubric will be general or task-specific. A general rubric is one that you use for a general performance-based assessment. For instance, if you are grading a research paper, there are certain traits you will be looking for in all research papers no matter what the topic: the content, the research, and the bibliography. No matter whether you are researching cancer treatments or the life of Walt Whitman, this rubric would serve as a general evaluator of any research paper. An example is shown in Figure 5.3.

Sometimes a PBA might not be so easy to generalize. Task-specific rubrics are used to determine a specific, measurable task. The task defines the rubric, and it would be difficult to use a task-specific rubric for another PBA unless the student is performing that specific task again. Figure 5.4 is an example of a task-based rubric.

The advantages of a general or specific rubric really come down to convenience. A general rubric can be used for several projects, so only a single one needs to be made. Students also become very familiar with the rubric if it is used multiple times, and they become familiar with the repeated expectations. A task-specific rubric allows you to focus on a very specific task you would like to evaluate. If you are doing a performance-based assessment that is very content heavy and you want to be sure specific content is being mastered by the students, use a task-specific rubric. This means having to create original rubrics from time to time, but you want to make sure the rubric is evaluating what you need it to.

The final decision you need to consider when making a rubric is how to score it. You can set up rubrics so that they award a certain number of points; such a rubric is shown in Figure 5.5. A teacher using this rubric would simply circle or fill in the

Question: Why was the river important to China and India? Be sure to explain your answer with examples and detail.	
Grade: A	Students need to specifically mention how the river would have helped each of the two civilizations. For instance, India used the river for a couple of specific purposes. One was for their sewage system. They used the water to take away the waste, which was a benefit because it prevented disease and the spreading of sickness. They also built bricks formed from the mud of the river, which they then put in the kilns they created to make stronger materials. China used the water for growing rice, which was a staple crop for them. More rice meant more food, which meant more people survived. Rice needs to be submerged in water, which they did using the water from the river to irrigate. Similarly, they used the water from the river for the purpose of crop rotation. This means leaving a field unused to allow it to build up nutrients. They would irrigate the fields but only use certain ones to allow the field to be useful the next year.
Grade: B	Same as above, but the student may only have a specific example for one of the two civilizations and a general one for the other. A general example would be mentioning farming without a specific farming method used or that the river was used for drinking water or bathing. The student may have provided many general, but not specific, examples and explained their importance with much detail.
Grade: C	The student provided many general examples, such as farming, drinking, bathing, etc., but didn't explain their importance to the civilizations. The student may have mentioned water for drinking but didn't fully explain how that would be beneficial to the civilization.
Grade: D	The student included only one or two examples and he/she was general. The student's explanations were very general or otherwise very confusing.
Grade: F	Some of the student's examples did not even match the civilizations, or the information was wholly incorrect.

Figure 5.1. Sample holistic rubric.

SHAKESPEARE LITERARY REPORT RUBRIC

Student: _____ Play: _____

	Compare/Contrast	Theme	Student Reaction	Mechanics
Excellent (A)	• Two plays are compared/contrasted using specific examples to illustrate the relationship between them. • The two literary terms are discussed in depth with detail and profound insight.	• Explains the theme of the play in an insightful and meaningful way. • Idea of power is addressed with detailed supporting examples.	• Demonstrates an in-depth opinion of the play. • Analyzes the quality/style of the literary work with appropriate examples and detail. • Gives a detailed and supported explanation to the timelessness of the play.	• Paragraphs have clear beginning, middle, and end sentences. • Uses correct word processing format. • Has few or no errors in spelling, grammar, or usage.
Good (B–C)	• Two plays are compared/contrasted using limited examples to illustrate the relationship between them. • The two literary terms are discussed in general.	• Explains the theme of the play in an adequate manner. • Idea of power is addressed with a basic supporting example.	• Gives a basic opinion of the play. • Partially analyzes the quality/style of the literary work, providing examples to back the analysis up. • Gives a somewhat supported explanation to the timelessness of the play.	• Paragraphs respond directly to the questions without clear topic sentences or clear transitions. • Has errors in word processing format. • Has many errors in spelling, grammar, or usage.
Needs Improvement (D–F)	• Two plays are compared/contrasted but there are no examples to illustrate the relationship between them. • The literary terms are not discussed, or only one of them is.	• Does not give a clear explanation of the theme(s) of the play. • Idea of power is mentioned but not backed up with an example, or it is not addressed at all.	• Shows an unsupported or no opinion of the play. • Little or no reference to the literary style. • Does not give a reasonable explanation as to the timelessness of the play.	• Paragraphs ramble or lack clear focus or have no topic sentences. • Paper is not word processed. • Errors in spelling, grammar, or usage interfere with the meaning of the paper.

Figure 5.2. Sample analytical rubric.

RESEARCH PAPER

Student:_____   Topic:_____

Overall	Content	Research	Bibliography
Excellent (A)	<ul><li>Paper follows the outline clearly, allowing the reader to know what is being discussed at any given time</li><li>Student gives plenty of examples to back up statements made in the paper.</li><li>Student provides much detail, explaining concepts and ideas so that the reader can gain a full understanding of what is being discussed.</li></ul>	<ul><li>Research is consistently put into student's own words, paraphrasing the information.</li><li>Student uses one or more books as resources for a good amount of information, citing it several times.</li><li>A primary source with direct quotes is used in the paper to add to its depth.</li></ul>	<ul><li>A complete bibliography in the correct formatting is included.</li><li>More than three resources are cited in the bibliography.</li><li>Citations are consistently used correctly throughout the entire paper.</li></ul>
Good (B–C)	<ul><li>Paper follows the outline, but doesn't always allow the reader to know what is being discussed at any given time.</li><li>Student gives examples to back up statements made in the paper in most places but not consistently.</li><li>Student provides detail, explaining concepts and ideas so that the reader can gain an understanding of what is being discussed, but content could be clearer.</li></ul>	<ul><li>Research is put into student's own words, paraphrasing the information, but occasionally using terms and phrases not his/her own.</li><li>Student uses one or more books as resources for a little bit of information, only citing it once or twice.</li><li>A primary source with direct quotes is used in the paper but does not add to its depth.</li></ul>	<ul><li>A bibliography is included but is not in the correct format.</li><li>Three resources are cited in the bibliography.</li><li>Citations are used correctly throughout the entire paper but are missing in a few spots where needed.</li></ul>
Needs Improvement (D–F)	<ul><li>Paper does not follow the outline, causing confusion about what is being discussed.</li><li>Student provides little to no examples to back up statements made in the paper.</li><li>Student does not provide much detail.</li></ul>	<ul><li>Research is many times not put into the student's own words, using terms and phrases not his/her own.</li><li>Student does not use any books as resources or does not cites them in the paper.</li><li>A primary source with direct quotes is not used in the paper.</li></ul>	<ul><li>A bibliography is not provided or is badly formatted.</li><li>There are fewer than three resources cited in the bibliography.</li><li>Citations are used incorrectly or are missing in many places where needed.</li></ul>

Figure 5.3. Sample general rubric.

INVENT A BETTER MOUSETRAP

Student: _____

Overall	Design	Model	Comparison
Excellent	▪ Design clearly takes you step by step with its instructions. ▪ Design is clearly labeled with measurements and parts. ▪ Design looks neat and professional.	▪ Model looks exactly like the design. ▪ Model is durable and built sturdily so it can last. ▪ Model works, trapping the mouse without harming it.	▪ Student clearly compares design with the design of the original mousetrap. ▪ Presents both advantages and disadvantages of both traps. ▪ Gives good detail and examples why one trap is better than the other.
Good	▪ Design shows reader how to make mousetrap, but skips steps, making it hard to reproduce. ▪ Design is labeled with measurements and parts, but details are missing in some places. ▪ Design looks neat and professional for the most part, but is sloppy in some places.	▪ Model looks similar to the design with only a couple of minor changes. ▪ Model is durable and built somewhat sturdily, but won't hold up for very long. ▪ Model works for the most part, trapping the mouse without harming it, but it has a few glitches.	▪ Student compares design with the design of the original trap, but the comparisons are not always accurate or easy to understand. ▪ Student presents advantages or disadvantages of the traps but not both. ▪ Student explains why one trap is better than the other, but does not include much detail or give examples.
Needs Improvement	▪ Design does not show how someone can make the trap, leaving many steps out. ▪ Design is not labeled with either measurements or parts. ▪ Design does not look neat and professional and is sloppy and difficult to see.	▪ Model looks nothing like the design. ▪ Model is not durable and would not last long. ▪ Model does not work, falls apart, or harms the mouse.	▪ Student does not compare design to that of the original mousetrap. ▪ Student does not present either advantages or disadvantages of either trap. ▪ Student does not explain why one trap is better than the other.

Figure 5.4. Sample task-specific rubric.

AUTOBIOGRAPHY PAPER RUBRIC

Student: _____

	Content	Artifacts	Mechanics
Excellent (9–10)	- Chapter 1: Family roots give substantial insight to student's family. - Chapter 2: Family culture clearly shows how student was impacted. - Chapter 3: Personal section describes family and unique set of interests. - Chapter 4: Shows significance of multicultural experiences.	- Artifacts give a clear explanation of family history. - Many different items are used (e.g., letters, documents, photos, etc.) - Artifacts section is well planned, neat, and aesthetically pleasing.	- Autobiography is written in a clear and neat format. - No spelling errors. - Correctly formatted bibliography.
Good (7–8)	- Chapter 1: Family roots gives a picture of student's family, but it seems like there are details missing. - Chapter 2: Family culture vaguely explains how student was impacted. - Chapter 3: Personal section only generally explains family and interests. - Chapter 4: Illustrates only a few details of multicultural experiences.	- Artifacts give a general overview of family history. - Items used are nearly all the same. - Artifacts section is not in any particular order, although it is organized.	- Autobiography has some formatting problems. - A few spelling errors. - Some technical errors in bibliography.
Needs Improvement (0–6)	- Chapter 1: Family roots do not paint a picture of student's family. - Chapter 2: Family culture does not give a clear picture of how student was impacted. - Chapter 3: Personal section is a hodgepodge of events that do not coherently explain family or interests. - Chapter 4: Does not include a multicultural experience.	- Artifacts do not give a sense of family history. - Limited items used. - Artifact section is disorganized and seems thrown together.	- Autobiography is not formatted correctly. - Spelling errors affect the flow of the paper. - Many problems with bibliography.

Total: _____ /100

Figure 5.5. Sample point-based rubric

number she is awarding as a grade. Once she finishes assigning numbers to all the categories on the rubric, she'll add it up to get the total score.

The teacher can also set up scoring rubrics to weight categories differently should she feel one task is more important than another. Figure 5.6 is what a rubric would look like if it were weighted. In this case, the colleague I got the rubric from, Abbee Mansfield, valued the content much more than the visual elements of the assessment, making content 40% of the total grade and the visual only 10%. If the teacher wanted to give an overall grade, she would have to adjust her total to take into account these percentages. Another way to approach the scoring of a rubric is to provide a holistic evaluation, whether that's through particular point delineation or a letter grade. Figure 5.7 is an example. For a rubric such as this, you would circle the appropriate grade for each category. How many of each that you circle determines the overall grade according to already-established criteria.

As the teacher, you have to decide which of the combinations you want to use based on the PBA itself. If you are grading an essay, you might need to focus on one trait, and thus a holistic rubric would work better than an analytical rubric. If the performance is unique, you would need to use a task-specific rubric rather than a general one. Maybe your school's grading system calls for more precise percentages, and thus a scoring rubric with points is going to translate better to the grading system than one based on a letter grade would. Let your PBA be your guide on how to best evaluate it.

CREATING YOUR RUBRICS

Once you have decided how you are going to build your rubric, you actually have to create it. What is the best way to do this? The best piece of advice I can give on this matter is the following three words: Keep it simple. Creating a rubric is not a terribly difficult task, but it can be. If you follow some basic rules and keep it simple though, rubrics do not have to be a daunting task. A sample blank rubric is provided in Figure 5.8.

Here are some basic parameters to think about when creating your rubric. According to Bernie Dodge and Nancy Pickett (2007), successful rubrics should:

- focus on measuring a stated objective (e.g., performance, behavior, or quality),
- use a range to rate performance, and
- contain specific performance characteristics arranged in levels indicating either the developmental sophistication of the strategy used or the degree to which a standard has been met.

Herman, Aschbacher, and Winters (1992) distinguish the following elements of a scoring rubric:

Students: _____   Concept: _____

MATH VIDEO RUBRIC

Overall	Content (40%)	Visual (10%)	Group Work (20%)	Presentation (30%)
Excellent (A)	▪ Song clearly conveys the mathematical concept group intended at a higher level of understanding. ▪ Uses multiple examples to demonstrate the concept. ▪ All information is accurate.	▪ The graphics and images are creative and contribute to the presentation of the concept. ▪ The graphics and images enhance key points by contributing to the concept explanation. ▪ All shots are in focus with smooth transitions.	▪ Group used class time wisely, always on task and getting goals accomplished. ▪ Considerable planning and practice are evident. ▪ Group divided tasks equally amongst itself, with every member pulling his or her weight.	▪ Video is between 3 and 5 minutes long. ▪ Words are clear and presented at the appropriate volume. ▪ Lyrics and images accurately match images in the video and the tone and pace of the song.
Good (B–C)	▪ Song conveys the mathematical concept at a surface level but not with much depth. ▪ Uses examples to demonstrate the concept but needs more for full understanding. ▪ Most information is accurate, but not all.	▪ The graphics and images in the video contribute to the presentation. ▪ The graphics and images help explain the concept. ▪ Most shots are in focus with smooth transitions.	▪ Group used class time wisely, but not always on task. ▪ Planning and practice are evident, but there are clear places where more planning would have benefitted the group. ▪ Group divided the tasks unevenly.	▪ Video is a little over 5 minutes or a little under 3 minutes. ▪ Most words are clear and the volume is good. ▪ Lyrics and images mostly match the images in the video and the tone and pace of the song.
Needs Improvement (D–F)	▪ Song does not clearly convey the mathematical concept group intended to. ▪ Does not use many examples to demonstrate the concept. ▪ Much of the information is inaccurate, causing confusion.	▪ The graphics and images are not creative, distracting from the presentation of the concept. ▪ The graphics and images do not enhance key points, actually causing confusion. ▪ Many shots are not in focus and transitions are awkward.	▪ Group did not always use class time wisely, frequently off task. ▪ Planning and preparation are not evident. ▪ One or two group members did all of the work.	▪ Video is short of 3 minutes or well over 5. ▪ Words are not clear and presented at a volume that is difficult to hear. ▪ Lyrics and images do not accurately match images in the video, causing the presentation to be awkward.

Figure 5.6. Sample weighted rubric (developed by Abbee Mansfield; used with permission).

	Needs Improvement	Good	Excellent
Originality/ Creativity	Performers are idle and show no enthusiasm. The song does not have rhythm or catchiness, and the lyrics are taken from another source.	The song is somewhat catching and some members of the group display enthusiasm. The song is original but not overly clever. A prop is used, but has a tenuous connection to the song.	The song is very catchy and original, even if the tune is from an existing song. The entire group is enthusiastic. The group uses a prop in a relevant and clever manner.
Completeness	Group fails to cover any aspect of the assignment. Interpretation is incorrect, and there is no chorus to sum up the central idea of the song.	Covers some of the assignment, but other parts are neglected. Chorus is not repeated or does not contain the bulk of the main idea.	Entire assignment is addressed with clarity. The chorus explains the main idea of the song and is repeated enough times.
Relevance/Quiz	The quiz does not have five questions, or the questions have little or nothing to do with the main ideas of the song. Quiz is too easy or too difficult.	The quiz has five questions, but some questions have little or nothing to do with the assignment. Some of the questions are not covered by the song, and questions are either too simple or too difficult.	All five of the questions deal with the main points of the assignment. All of the questions are covered by the song, and the quiz is neither too difficult nor to easy.
Understandability/ Lyric Sheet	The lyrics are impossible to understand because the music is too loud or the words are spoken too quickly. No lyric sheet is provided, or it is not legible.	Some of the lyrics are hard to hear or do not make sense. Lyric sheet does not contain all of the lyrics, or some parts of it are hard to read.	All of the lyrics are clear and easy to understand. They lyric sheet is either typed or neatly written.

Figure 5.7. Sample holistic evaluation.

Figure 5.8. Sample blank rubric.

- one or more traits or dimensions that serve as the basis for judging the student response,
- definitions and examples to clarify the meaning of each trait or dimension,
- a scale of values on which to rate each dimension, and
- standards of excellence for specified performance levels accompanied by models or examples of each level.

Figure 5.9 is the basic template for any rubric you create. It has a place for the stated objective, the range of the performance, and the specific performance characteristics. You could certainly have more ranges, more objectives, and more specific performance characteristics, but in the spirit of keeping it simple, keep it at three.

There are six simple steps to creating a rubric:

1. Decide the range of performance.
2. Create categories.
3. Provide descriptors in each category.
4. Have a tiered system to the descriptors.
5. Make sure descriptors are specific and not vague.
6. Check the rubric over.

The first step is to decide the range of performance. As stated before, keep it simple. The more ranges, categories, and descriptors you have, the more you spread yourself thin while trying to consider which one each applies to. If you evaluate a PBA that is a physical performance happening right in front of you, you will have to have the ability to evaluate and assess fairly quickly. Too many categories will slow you down. Two is too few in that you basically give the student the option to either pass or fail. You may want to have more options than that. Figure 5.10 shows three simple ranges of performance. The ranges of performance have been divided into "excellent," "good," and "needs improvement." I like this range, especially for gifted students, because it allows you as the teacher to push students to the next level. I always tell students, "If you do everything that is required of you for this performance-based assessment, you did a good job. If you want to do an excellent job, you have to do something extra, something that makes it stand out from the others."

The second step is to create categories. You should decide how many overall categories you want to evaluate—usually no less than two and no more than four. Then, decide the weight of each category.

Figure 5.11 shows a rubric with categories. In this case, the teacher has decided to create a task-specific rubric. For this unit concerning the five themes of geography, the teacher determined the three categories he wanted to focus on: content, presentation, and maps. The teacher has enough categories to break down the overall performance-based assessment, but not so many that it is impossible to keep up with the presentation.

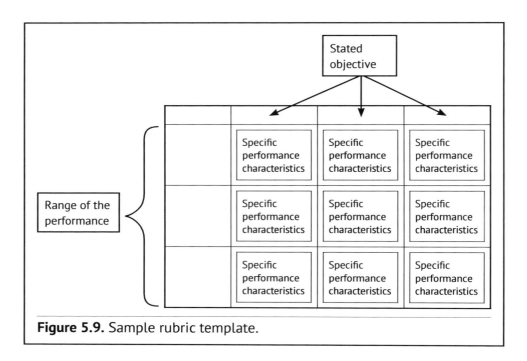

Figure 5.9. Sample rubric template.

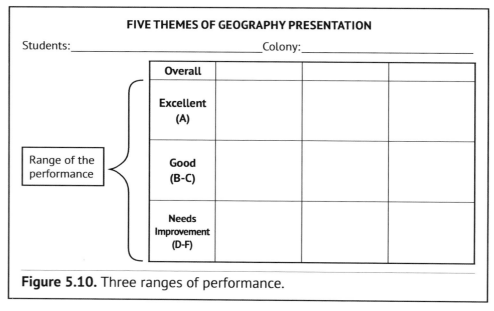

Figure 5.10. Three ranges of performance.

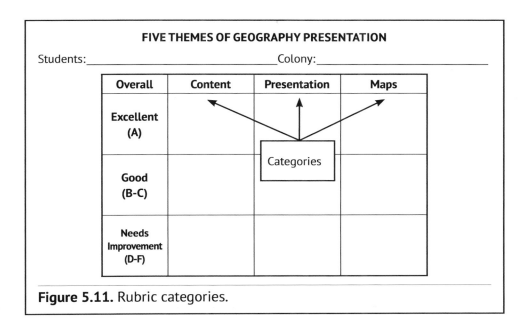

Figure 5.11. Rubric categories.

Step three is to provide descriptors for each of the categories chosen. Each category should have two to four skills being evaluated, which allows the evaluation to be more objective. Figure 5.12 offers an example. For content, the student knows she will need to focus on three aspects in order to be considered excellent: She will have to include many details and examples for each of the five themes of geography, make sure the research is accurate, and explain clearly how the borders of the colony came to be. This is a blueprint for the student. If she constructs her PBA using these descriptors, she can guarantee herself an excellent rating in this category.

Once the bar has been set in the "excellent" range for this category, it simply becomes a matter of showing what a PBA looks like when it is only "good" or when it "needs improvement." The content of the descriptor is the exact same, but the level at which the student achieves is different. That is where step four comes into play: creating the tier system for the other ranges in the category. Figure 5.13 is an example of a tiered system I've used in my own classroom.

Things you should consider when creating this tiered system are:

- Each category should have a matching descriptor at each level. In other words, the skill being assessed should be described on all levels of the range.
- Each level should be realistic. The highest range should have high expectations and the lowest should reflect poor quality work.
- Number the levels so students can see the correlation between them more clearly.

The simplest way I have found to do this is by using the term "but" for the middle range and "not" for the lowest. For example:

FIVE THEMES OF GEOGRAPHY PRESENTATION

Students:_____Colony:_____

Overall	Content	Presentation	Maps
Excellent (A)	▪ Includes many details and examples designed to back up each of the five themes of geography. ▪ Research is accurate and gives a clear picture of the theme it is supposed to be demonstrating. ▪ Explains clearly and with much detail how the borders of the colony came to be.	Descriptors	
Good (B-C)			
Needs Improvement (D-F)			

Figure 5.12. Rubric descriptors.

- Excellent: Includes many details and examples designed to back up each of the five themes of geography.
- Good: Has a few details and examples to back up five themes *but* could use more.
- Needs Improvement: Does *not* use details and examples to back up the five themes.

Keep in mind these descriptors need to be very clear so that students can follow them. Sometimes it is difficult to break down a performance-based assessment into parts like this but if the teacher cannot do it, how can he expect the students to be able to do the same?

A problem you want to avoid is using the word "some" in your descriptors, such as "includes *some* maps." The problem with the word "some" is that it is very vague and is subject to much interpretation. Technically, $2 is *some* money, and so is $100. But there is a vast difference between those two sums. Furthermore, the student definition of "some" and the teacher definition might be very different. A student might define "some" maps as three, but the teacher might be thinking this means seven. Rather than having the student try to guess what the teacher might mean, the teacher should use a specific range for the sake of clarity. This can be seen in the final rubric for the five themes of geography, shown in Figure 5.14. An "excellent" amount of maps is clearly defined as 10 or more in the maps category; "good" consists of seven to nine maps,

FIVE THEMES OF GEOGRAPHY PRESENTATION

Students:_____Colony:_____

Overall	Content	Presentation	Maps
Excellent (A) Tiered	1. Includes many details and examples to back up the five themes of geography. 2. Research is accurate and gives a clear picture of the theme it is supposed to be demonstrating. 3. Explains clearly and with much detail how the borders of the colony came to be.		
Good (B–C) [But]	1. Has a few details and examples to back up five themes but could use more. 2. Research is accurate but does not give a clear picture of the theme, showing one aspect rather than a well-rounded picture. 3. Explains how the borders of the colony came to be but does not provide much detail.		
Needs Improvement (D–F) [not]	1. Does not use details and examples to back up the five themes. 2. Research is inaccurate, giving the audience the wrong idea about the themes. 3. Does not explain very well how the borders came to be where they are.		

Figure 5.13. Tiered system.

and six or fewer would mean the assessment "needs improvement." These standards are clearly defined so there is no confusion or guesswork on the part of the student.

When doing a performance-based assessment for the first time, it can be difficult to envision what the final product is going to look like. Creating a usable rubric can be a challenge. Here are some tips to ensure that the rubric will be a successful one:

- Go through each category and check each tier to be sure it flows and makes sense.
- Practice grading a performance and see how practical the rubric is.
- Have students or another teacher look the rubric over for any mistakes they might find. It always helps to have a set of fresh eyes. You could even go over it as a class—this will help establish the expectations.

FIVE THEMES OF GEOGRAPHY PRESENTATION

Students: _____   Colony: _____

Overall	Content	Presentation	Maps
Excellent (A)	▪ Includes many details and examples designed to back up each of the five themes of geography. ▪ Research is accurate and gives a clear picture of the theme it is supposed to be demonstrating. ▪ Explains clearly and with much detail how the borders of the colony came to be.	▪ Presentation has a flow to it with each person's role clearly defined. Planning and preparation are evident. ▪ Presentation uses meaningful visuals that add to the content. ▪ Speakers present clearly; do not read the presentation to the audience.	▪ Includes at least 10 maps that show the various themes of geography. ▪ Maps can easily be seen by the audience. ▪ Maps clearly explain what they are showing.
Good (B–C)	▪ Has a few details and examples to back up five themes but could use more. ▪ Research is accurate but does not give a clear picture of the theme, showing one aspect rather than a well-rounded picture. ▪ Explains how the borders of the colony came to be but does not provide much detail.	▪ Presentation jumps around a little, making it difficult to follow. ▪ Presentation uses visuals but not all of them are meaningful. ▪ Speakers present clearly most of the time but every once in a while read the presentation to the class.	▪ Includes seven to nine maps that show the themes of geography but could use a few more. ▪ Most maps can be easily seen by the audience, but a few are not clear. ▪ Most maps include explanations, but others are not discussed in detail.
Needs Improvement (D–F)	▪ Does not use details and examples to back up the five themes. ▪ Research is inaccurate, giving the audience the wrong information. ▪ Does not explain very well how the borders came to be.	▪ Presentation is so unorganized it is difficult to tell what is being taught. ▪ Presentation lacks visuals, or visuals add nothing to content. ▪ Speakers read the entire presentation and do not make themselves heard.	▪ Includes six or fewer maps, or no maps that contain meaningful information. ▪ Maps cannot be easily seen by the audience. ▪ Many of the maps are not properly explained and act as background visuals.

Figure 5.14. Final rubric.

HOW TO MAKE YOUR RUBRICS MORE VALID AND OBJECTIVE

When creating the rubric, you want to be sure first and foremost that it is valid—in other words, that it's measuring what it needs to be measuring. You want reliable results, but sometimes this is difficult to discern when you are working on a performance-based assessment for the first time.

There are five characteristics all valid rubrics have. If you run your rubric through this checklist, the rubric should be as objective as it can be (Baker, O'Neill, & Linn, 1993). The rubric should:

1. Have meaning for students and teachers and motivate high performance.
2. Require the demonstration of complex cognition.
3. Exemplify current standards of content or subject matter quality.
4. Minimize the effects of ancillary skills that are irrelevant to the focus of assessment.
5. Possess explicit standards for rating or judgment. (p. 1212)

In order for the rubric to have meaning and to motivate high performance, it is important to go over the rubric with students. It is even better if you can have the students use the rubric to evaluate a performance. We talked in an earlier chapter about modeling performance-based assessment or showing students examples from past classrooms. It is always a good idea to have the students take the rubric out for a test drive of their own. For example, show students a video of a past performance and place a copy of the rubric in front of them, asking them to evaluate the performance. Then as a class, go over the general consensus of the performance. What did students choose when it came to their evaluation and what justification did they have for choosing it? Make sure you share with students how you evaluated this performance yourself. This will help students to see how the rubric is used. It will bring meaning to the rubric. If you do not have a past performance, model the performance for them yourself and have them evaluate you.

Make sure you stop and have conversations about what made something fall into the top range of performance and what could have been done to improve one that was given a lower grade. This will clearly demonstrate to the students what they have to do to achieve that top level of performance.

Rubrics should be able to measure the demonstration of complex cognition, not just rudimentary skills. This is especially important for gifted students. It can sometimes be tough to measure this higher level of thinking, so constructing objective descriptors for your rubric is important. For example, if you want to determine whether students understood a concept at a higher level, you can use the tier system shown in Figure 5.15.

Deeper Understanding	▪ Student appears to grasp the concept at a higher level of thinking and is able to use it in another context. ▪ Student gives plenty of original examples not used in class to illustrate a deeper understanding of the concept. ▪ Student goes above and beyond in the depth of the explanation, providing insights that show a deeper understanding of the concept.
Surface-Level Understanding	▪ Student appears to have a surface-level understanding of the concept but has difficulty using it in another context. ▪ Student gives examples used in class to back up a basic understanding but does not appear able to create any original examples. ▪ Student covers the concept with a workmanlike explanation but does not add any insights that would show a deeper understanding.
Lack of Understanding	▪ Student does not appear to grasp the basic concept, using it incorrectly and is not able to use it in another context. ▪ Student provides little to no examples, or the examples used are not linked clearly to the concept. ▪ Student seems to miss what the concept is about, misunderstanding how and why it is used.

Figure 5.15. Higher level tier system.

This rubric allows a teacher to evaluate whether a student reached those higher levels of complex cognition by determining whether original examples were used, whether the student used the concept in another concept, and whether the explanation is insightful or not. Objective multiple-choice tests do not really allow for this. Even if the students get one answer correct that demonstrates a higher understanding, there is always the chance the student guessed. It is not possible to guess on a performance-based assessment.

In order to exemplify current standards of content, it is important to link performance-based assessments to Common Core State Standards. You can evaluate such performance-specific skills such as informative PowerPoint presentations, effective public speaking, and relevant use of visuals, but the meat of your evaluation will probably need to be linked to a particular Common Core standard. It is recommended that one of your categories be dedicated to the Common Core standard you are having students demonstrate so that you can ensure the grade for that category reflects whether or not the student truly mastered it. You do not want to give a student a glowing grade because her speaking ability was excellent and her professionalism was adequate if she did not demonstrate an understanding of the CCSS you intended for her to master.

Here is a content statement that needs to be mastered in the fifth grade in social studies concerning the Native Americans (Ohio's New Learning Standards, 2012):

> American Indians developed unique cultures with many different ways of life. American Indian tribes and nations can be classified into cultural groups based on geographic and cultural similarities. (p. 11)

The standard indicates that the Native American culture needs to be the important concept mastered by students in this unit, which also needs to be reflected in the PBA. Figure 5.16 is a sample rubric for a lesson concerning Native American culture that I used in my own class. The standard covered in the assignment for students to demonstrate is how environment shapes culture. The emphasis of this was placed on the weighting of the grade and was mentioned several times in the project description. It was stated in the assignment very clearly that students could not pass this PBA with just a professional-looking artifact and a snazzy display. There had to be some substance to their style. The "excellent" range was clearly defined in the rubric and stated that the assessment should:

- explain an aspect of Native American culture in detail,
- explain with examples how the environment shaped this particular aspect of culture, and
- include original research in the content that teaches the audience how the Native Americans used this aspect of culture.

Linking the CCSS to the rubric is paramount to making the performance-based assessment legitimate. Although a student gaining 21st-century skills is valuable in the classroom, we must not forget the content our students will be accountable for. You have to be careful when creating your rubric that you do not focus on skills that don't determine content and standard mastery. Let us again use the Native American assessment as an example. Consider if Figure 5.17 had been the rubric used instead of the one shared in Figure 5.16. The categories of artifact, display, and research, although important to the museum exhibition, are ancillary to the overall goal of students mastering how environment affects Native American culture. This should be the focus of the assessment and yet it is not evaluated anywhere in the rubric. It is easy for the students to lose sight of this focus as they get caught up in the more artistic aspects of the PBA. It is important that the teacher be the shining beacon that keeps students' focus on the main idea throughout the assessment.

If you make sure your rubric descriptors are specific and not vague, you will go a long way in making the rubric more objective. One strategy to make sure the rubric is more objective is to anchor grade a few performances. This might mean inviting multiple people to use the rubric in evaluating a performance-based assessment. You could invite other teachers, administrators, parents, or even students. Once the performance

Overall	Artifact	Display	Content
Excellent (A)	▪ Artifact looks professional. ▪ Artifact clearly captures the aspect of the culture it is meant to. ▪ Artifact is easy for people to view, showing many details about the aspect of the culture.	▪ Display has an appropriate title that clearly captures what the artifact is about as well as the viewer's attention. ▪ Display is written clearly so that it is easy to read. ▪ Display is free of spelling errors and looks professional.	▪ Aspect of culture is explained in detail. ▪ Student explains with examples how the environment shaped this particular aspect of culture. ▪ There is obvious research in the content, teaching the reader how the Native Americans used this aspect of culture.
Good (B–C)	▪ Artifact looks somewhat professional, like a good-quality school project. ▪ Artifact captures most of the aspect of the culture it is meant to but leaves some parts out. ▪ Artifact can be viewed by many but some details are difficult to see.	▪ Display has a general title that captures what the artifact is about but does not capture the viewer's attention. ▪ Display is written clearly for the most part, but there are sections that are not as easy to read. ▪ Display has just a couple of spelling errors and looks professional.	▪ Aspect of the culture is explained but lacks detail in places where it is needed. ▪ Student explains how the environment shaped this particular aspect of culture but does not provide clear examples. ▪ There is a little research in the content, but does not clearly teach the reader how the Native Americans used this aspect of culture.
Needs Improvement (D–F)	▪ Artifact does not look professional, like something an elementary student would make. ▪ Artifact does not capture the aspect of culture it is meant to, causing confusion. ▪ Artifact is not easy for people to view, leaving out many details about the aspect of culture.	▪ Display does not have an appropriate title or has no title at all. ▪ Display is not written clearly, making it difficult to read. ▪ Display is full of spelling errors and/or does not look professional.	▪ Aspect of culture is not well explained, causing confusion. ▪ Student does not explain how the environment shaped this particular aspect of culture or explains incorrectly. ▪ There is no research in the content, failing to teach the reader how the Native Americans used this aspect of culture.
Weight	20%	10%	70%

Figure 5.16. Native American rubric 1.

NATIVE AMERICAN MUSEUM

Overall	Artifact	Display	Research
Excellent (A)	▪ Artifact looks professional, like something that would be on display in a museum. ▪ Artifact clearly captures the aspect of culture it is meant to. ▪ Artifact is easy for people to view, showing many details about the aspect of culture.	▪ Display has an appropriate title that clearly captures what the artifact is about as well as the viewer's attention. ▪ Display is written clearly so that it is easy to read. ▪ Display is free of spelling errors and looks professional.	▪ Research is consistently put into a student's own words. ▪ Student uses specific facts and data where necessary, giving the reader a clear picture. ▪ Student uses one or more books as resources for a good amount of information, citing it several times.
Good (B–C)	▪ Artifact looks somewhat professional, like a good-quality school project. ▪ Artifact captures most of the aspect of culture it is meant to but leaves some parts out. ▪ Artifact can be viewed by many but some details are difficult to see.	▪ Display has a general title that captures what the artifact is about but does not capture the viewer's attention. ▪ Display is written clearly for the most part, but there are sections that are not as easy to read. ▪ Display has just a couple of spelling errors and looks professional.	▪ Research is put into student's own words, but occasionally the student uses terms and phrases directly from other sources. ▪ Student uses facts and data but may not be very specific or not where needed. ▪ Student uses one or more books as resources for a little bit of information, citing only once or twice.
Needs Improvement (D–F)	▪ Artifact does not look professional, like something an elementary student would make. ▪ Artifact does not capture the aspect of culture it is meant to, causing confusion. ▪ Artifact is not easy for people to view, leaving out many details about the aspect of culture.	▪ Display does not have an appropriate title or no title at all. ▪ Display is not written clearly, making it difficult to read. ▪ Display is full of spelling errors and/or does not look professional.	▪ Research is often not put into a student's words; student seems to have lifted information directly from other sources. ▪ Student does not use facts and data where necessary, leaving the viewer/reader with more questions than answers. ▪ Student does not use books as sources or never cites them in the display.

Figure 5.17. Native American rubric 2.

is over, you compare how each of you evaluated the performance. If the range is similar, such as all three evaluators rating the performance as "good," then you know the rubric is most likely objective. If, however, one person gives the performance a "needs improvement" while another sees it as "excellent," there is too much subjectivity in how the rubric is worded and needs to be more specific. Anchoring is a good way to make sure the standards for judgment are explicit and as objective as possible.

CREATING RUBRICS WITH STUDENTS

One way to have students even more invested in a rubric is to create the rubric together as a class. When a teacher gives a rubric to students at the beginning of a PBA, students might glance at it or maybe even leave it behind when the bell rings. By creating the rubric as a class, the students are more aware of what is in it because they contributed to its content.

In order to do this, follow the same six steps used when creating your own rubric, but have the students help create the range, categories, and descriptors. Having students come up with the categories allows them to break down the performance-based assessment so that they can see for themselves what components make a successful PBA. This especially helps those students who have trouble seeing the big picture. The dialogue of a class debate on what is a valid descriptor and what is not is also very enlightening because students become very clear on how they will be evaluated.

Although you as the teacher are leading the discussion, sitting back and letting the students arrive at conclusions for themselves and deciding what makes for different ranges of grades can be very powerful. In most cases, students will arrive at the same decisions you would have made yourself, but in this scenario, they feel as though they were made part of the process. This allows them to connect to the entire evaluation process.

I got to the point in my science class where I needed many different rubrics. Instead of making all of these myself, I trained my students to create their own rubrics. In order to gain approval to move forward on a project, they had to have a contract, a calendar, and a rubric. I had students for 2 years at a time, and by the end of those 2 years, they grew quite adept at making rubrics. I even had them lead a teacher workshop for the staff on how to make a valid rubric. The skill of making a really good, objective rubric is something that can be taught to learners of all ages.

SUMMARY

According to H. Goodrich (1996), in order to use rubrics effectively in the classroom you must have the following criteria:

1. Have students look at models of good versus "not-so-good" work. A teacher could provide sample assignments of variable quality for students to review.

2. List the criteria to be used in the scoring rubric and allow for discussion of what counts as quality work. Asking for student feedback during the creation of the list also allows the teacher to assess the students' overall writing experiences.

3. Articulate gradations of quality. These hierarchical categories should concisely describe the levels of quality (ranging from bad to good) or development (ranging from beginning to mastery). They can be based on the discussion of the good versus not-so-good work samples or immature versus developed samples. Using a conservative number of gradations keeps the scoring rubric user friendly while allowing for fluctuations that exist within the average range.

4. Practice on models. Students can test the scoring rubrics on sample assignments provided by the instructor. This practice can build students' confidence by teaching them how the instructor would use the scoring rubric on their papers. It can also aid student/teacher agreement on the reliability of the scoring rubric.

5. Ask for self- and peer-assessment.

6. Revise the work on the basis of that feedback. As students are working on their assignment, they can be stopped occasionally to do a self-assessment and then give and receive evaluations from their peers. Revisions should be based on the feedback they receive.

7. Use teacher assessments, which means using the same scoring rubric the students used to assess their work (pp. 14–16).

Everything on this list has been discussed in some form or another in this chapter with exception to self- and peer assessment, which we will talk about in the next chapter on making your assessment authentic.

Based on the criteria in this list, it would be safe to assume that if you follow the steps laid out for you in this chapter, you will be able to create rubrics that evaluate PBA in your classroom in an objective manner.

CHAPTER 6

How to Make the Performance-Based Assessment Authentic

Performance-based assessments by nature should be authentic. What helps with this is a formula. Like most formulas, it is not about throwing random variables in and hoping for the best. You have to make sure you have the proper variables and that they are quality ones. The basic formula for authentic learning is the sum of four aspects (Rule, 2006):

- real-world problems,
- higher level thinking,
- a community of learners, and
- student-directed learning (p. 1).

You may have used these aspects in various forms in the past. A math teacher trying to teach students how to balance a checkbook is employing a real-world problem. A science teacher asking students to conduct their own experiment and analyze the data using the scientific method is having students think at a higher level. A social studies teacher having students work in groups to create a mural has engaged them in a community of learners. And an English teacher who allows students to choose which books they will read is involved in student-directed learning. Some teachers may even use two or three of these aspects at the same time, but it is the combination of all four of them that makes for the ideal authentic classroom.

REAL-WORLD PROBLEMS

Using real-world problems involves taking the content you have to teach and connecting it to a real-world situation. That connection is more than having students solve a word problem that involves a real-world situation. It means actually having students produce a product that could be used in the real world or that simulates a real-world situation.

If you are trying to teach students persuasive writing, have them write letters to congressmen or newspaper editors about an issue they feel strongly about rather than an arbitrary essay no one but the teacher is going to read. Or rather than reading about ecosystems in their science book, have students study the ecosystems that exist in their backyards or around the school in order to create a 3-D food web or chain. Instead of learning about economics by analyzing companies, have students research their town and come up with a plan for a business they would open in the community. Performance-based assessment by its very definition allows the teacher to put the lesson in the real world because it calls for action. Be sure to make this action wrought with real-world implications that simulate a real-world situation. This will enable students to make more of a connection and understand the context of how school fits into everyday life.

A simple way to bring a PBA into the real world is to have a real-world evaluation. This could involve having outside experts come in and act as a panel for the evaluation of the performance. This does a few things:

- It immediately makes the assessment more real for the students. It is one thing to give a presentation to fellow classmates or even a teacher, but when someone from the outside community comes in to evaluate, it ups the ante for students.
- It develops those 21st-century public speaking skills even more. If a the panel is made up of experts, the students will have to be more professional and less casual than if they were just doing a school assignment in front of classmates. I have seen time and time again students really stepping up their game when they are in front of people they deem to be experts.
- It provides an additional perspective. As much as we as teachers try to be experts on everything, it is an impossible task. Bringing in an engineer to evaluate student toothpick bridges or having the mayor listen to students give political speeches provides a level of expertise that is valuable. These experts are going to be able to offer their own experiences and share a perspective that you won't be able to.

If you are going to have outside experts evaluate students, you need to have rubrics for them to assess with. One piece of advice I would give is that even though these guest evaluators may be experts in their given fields, they are not necessarily teachers.

Providing them with a simple rubric that allows them to evaluate students properly is important. And explaining to the evaluators how a rubric works also goes a long way in getting meaningful feedback for students. You might even simplify the options an evaluator can grade students on. This would need to be explained to students at the beginning of the PBA so that there are no surprises. This makes the grading process easier and more objective for the evaluators.

There are even times when using parents as the evaluator can be an effective approach. I once assigned a PBA where students had to create a budget for their lives based on a base salary. Students had to come up with where they would live, utilities, food costs, and other monthly living expenses. For the final evaluation, rather than having me evaluate them, I had students present their portfolios to their parents. This opened up real-world conversations between students and parents about what the parents paid monthly on regular expenses and how they budgeted their money. Parents had to evaluate using a simple rubric, shown in Figure 6.1, which simplified the choices down to a single descriptor.

No matter how you decide to connect your performance-based assessment to the real world, it is a necessary step to making it authentic.

HIGHER LEVEL THINKING

The next criteria to making your PBA authentic is making sure students are employing higher level thinking in order to master the assessment. We saw in an earlier chapter on how using Bloom's taxonomy and higher level cue words can be an easy way to foster critical thinking. This can come in a couple of forms, the first of which is a prompt for writing. The teacher provides the prompt, to which the students must respond in written form. Most times, this takes the shape of an essay. The teacher takes the content-based, lower level questions and rewrites them so that they are higher level questions, or adds additional prompts that take the lower level content into a higher level of thinking.

Some Common Core standards are written in such a way that they are already at a higher level of thinking, so creating a higher level question should be easy (National Governors Association Center for Best Practices & Council of Chief State Officers, 2010b):

> CCSS.Math.Content 6.NS.C.7B: Write, interpret, and explain statements of order for rational numbers in real-world contexts.

CCSS of this variety are perfect for performance-based assessments given their emphasis on higher level, critical thinking. Other times the standard is written at a lower level but you as the teacher can alter the question to encourage more criti-

ECONOMIC PORTFOLIO RUBRIC

Student: _____   Parent: _____

Directions: Please circle the grade you feel your child deserves for each of the four categories along with a brief justification for your choice. Then, circle the overall grade you feel he/she deserves for the portfolio. Thanks for your help with this.

Overall	Content	Organization	Rationale	Requirements
Excellent (A)	▪ Covers topic in depth with details and examples. Subject knowledge is excellent.	▪ Content is well organized, using headings and appropriately used bulleted lists to group related material.	▪ All decisions are fully explained and justified. Impact of choices has been explicitly addressed.	▪ All requirements are met and exceeded.
Good (B)	▪ Includes essential knowledge about the topic. Subject knowledge appears to be good, but there are one to two factual errors.	▪ Uses headings and bulleted lists to organize, but the overall organization of topics appears flawed.	▪ Most decisions are explained and justified. Some impact has been considered.	▪ All requirements are met.
Average (C)	▪ Includes essential information about the topic, but there are three to four factual errors.	▪ Content is logically organize for the most part.	▪ Some decisions are explained and justified.	▪ One or two requirements were not completely met.
Needs Improvement (D–F)	▪ Content is minimal OR there are five or more factual errors.	▪ There is no clear or logical organizational structure, just a bundle of facts.	▪ Very few if any decisions were explained and/or justified.	▪ Three or more requirements were not completely met.

Figure 6.1. Simple rubric with single descriptors.

cal thinking. Here is an example of the progression of a higher level essay question from its origins as a lower level Common Core standard (Association Center for Best Practices & Council of Chief State School Officers, 2010a):

CCSS.ELA-Literacy.RL.4.2: Determine the theme of a story, drama, or poem from details in the text; summarize the text.

A teacher could take this CCSS and turn it into the following essay question: *What is the theme of "Goldilocks and the Three Bears"? Make sure to use details from the text to support this choice.* This is a fairly serviceable essay question that certainly captures the mastery intended in the CCSS and requires students to think at a lower level. This question at best would ask the students to work at the low level of application, where they take their understanding of what a theme is and apply it to the content of "Goldilocks and the Three Bears." In order to take this to a higher level of thinking, the teacher would need to include an additional prompt to challenge the students to think critically. This additional prompt would need to use language that requires students to think on the levels of analyzing, evaluating, or creating. Here is what that would look like:

What is the theme of "Goldilocks and the Three Bears"? Make sure to use details from the text to support this choice. "Goldilocks and the Three Bears" was written nearly 200 years ago. Justify whether this theme applies to today. Provide an example from modern life to validate your answer.

With the addition of the words "justify" and "validate," we have now asked students to think at the evaluation and the analysis levels, both higher levels of thinking than mere application.

You can also arrange your essay questions to scaffold into higher level thinking. Start with a lower level question to get students aware of the content, and then ask additional questions that take that basic knowledge to a higher level of thinking. Here is an example of a social studies PBA that scaffolds:

- Why was the Huang Ho River important to ancient China? Be sure to explain your answer with examples and detail.
- Compare and contrast **one** of the following topics between ancient China and modern-day society (e.g., gender roles, government, religion, class structure). Be sure to explain your comparisons clearly with evidence to back them up.
- Name two contributions that ancient China gave to the world, why they were important to their civilization, and their importance to modern-day society.

The first question asks for the lower level skill of recalling examples of why the Huang Ho River was important to ancient China. The second question asks for recall of the attributes of an aspect in ancient Chinese culture, and the comparison/contrast part of the question requires an analysis of the topic. Similarly, the third question requires the recall of two contributions and an analysis of why they were important to ancient China, but also an evaluation of what made those contributions important in the context of history. The questions started at a lower level and were scaffolded up to more advanced critical thinking.

In a performance-based assessment where there is not a written performance, the higher level questioning comes in the learning outcome you want students to achieve. Say, for instance, that students are working on a performance-based assessment concerning science. You want students to be able to master the following learning objective:

> Identify the three different types of rock—metamorphic, sedimentary, and igneous—using their characteristics.

You want to create a PBA that requires students to think at a higher level because simply identifying is a lower level application skill. You need to change the learning objective so that students will have to achieve a higher level of thinking in order to master it:

> Classify 20 different rocks you find around your neighborhood. Label the rocks as metamorphic, sedimentary, or igneous based on their characteristics and explain how you identified them. Analyze the types of rocks you find and infer what in the environment you live in would create such rocks.

The classification and explanation of how students identified rocks are all in the realm of application, a lower level skill. Analyzing and making inferences about how these rocks formed in their environments, however, takes the skill to an analytical realm and requires a higher level of thinking.

In addition to the thinking skills involved in executing the essay or learning objective is the process involved in creating the performance. This process may require several thinking skills, many of which are higher level (Glencoe/McGraw-Hill, 2000):

- Getting information (i.e., finding, completing, counting, collecting, reading, listening, defining, describing, identifying, listing, matching, naming, observing, recording, reciting, selecting, scanning).
- Working with the information (i.e., comparing, contrasting, classifying, sorting, distinguishing, explaining why, inferring, sequencing, analyzing, synthe-

sizing, generalizing, evaluating, making analogies, making models, and/or reasoning).

- Using information for a purpose (i.e., informing, persuading, motivating).
- Using information to craft a product/presentation (i.e., speaking, debating, singing, writing, surveying, designing, drawing, computing, constructing, demonstrating, acting out).
- Using information to communicate with specific audiences (i.e., such as peers, younger, older, informed, uninformed, friendly, hostile, apathetic, homogeneous, or diverse groups). (para. 12)

Let us continue with the example of students identifying rocks. You could make the process of creating the product require a higher level of thinking but keep the mastery of the content skill at the originally intended level:

> Create a game (e.g., board game, card game, computer game, etc.) in which players need to be able to identify different types of rocks using their characteristics. An example of this would be a game called "Rock, Rock, Rock" based on Rock, Paper, Scissors, in which players would be an igneous, a metamorphic, or sedimentary rock. There would be cards with various types of rocks that players would use to play with. Sedimentary rocks beat igneous rocks because weathering and erosion cause igneous rocks to turn into sedimentary rocks. Metamorphic rocks beat sedimentary rocks because pressure causes sedimentary rocks to turn into metamorphic rocks. And igneous rocks beat metamorphic rocks because when the former melt and cool, they become metamorphic, all based on the rock cycle.

In this PBA, students are still mastering the skill of being able to identify rocks using their characteristics, but by creating a game that others must understand and play, they are using higher levels of thinking and even get to be creative in how they make their game. The content skill is still a lower level one, but the assessment students create requires the use of higher level 21st-century skills.

Whether creating essay questions or a learning outline, recognizing appropriate prompts to generate higher level questioning is a good skill to possess as a teacher of gifted students. There are more examples of these prompts in the appendix.

COMMUNITY OF LEARNERS

When using PBA in the classroom, a teacher should take every opportunity to have students working together. Yes, this means dreaded group work, the bane of many teachers' existence. There are some disadvantages to group work, including:

- unequal participation,
- members who are not team players,
- time-consuming activities,
- weakening strong ideas for the sake of a compromise, and
- conflict between personalities.

Most of these problems occur when the classroom structure is not sound and group work has not been purposely taught. If you put together a bunch of students without any direction or guidance, you are bound to run into the problems listed above just as you would run into problems if you grouped random adults together. When you have students work in a community of learners, you have to be deliberate about the skills you teach about how to learn in a cooperative setting as well as make each individual member of the group accountable. When group work is done successfully, it is an authentic skill and is highly valued in the real world. What business would not want an employee with strong interpersonal skills? Specifically, businesses want an employee who can (Glencoe/McGraw-Hill, 2000):

- establish and maintain positive working relationships within/outside the employees' group,
- work toward departmental goals,
- work well in a team environment, and
- display an ability/willingness to understand viewpoints of others. (para. 15)

In short, businesses want someone who is a team player and can work successfully with others, a 21st-century skill if there ever was one. This is why it is important to use cooperative learning in the classroom. Cooperative learning also causes students to give greater thought to time management, organizing and prioritizing tasks, and goal setting—also 21st-century skills. Greater thought must be put into group activities because decisions are not being made or carried out by a single person, but by a group that includes many perspectives and ideas that must be considered.

In order to teach purposeful collaborative learning, one strategy is the use of norms. This means there are agreed-upon expectations of the group. This goes a long way in solving conflicts and making sure all group members participate. Another strategy that can be used when students are working in groups is the use of peer evaluations. These are grades meted out by each student rating the effort of the group members. In order for these peer evaluations to have an effect, they must include the overall grade. When I am doing a PBA where students are working in groups, the content is worth 75% of the grade, with peer evaluations making up another 25%. What typically happens is one student works really hard but the group receives a C on the content of the performance. However, on the peer evaluations, the group awards that student with an A because she worked really hard and contributed the most to the performance. This will raise her overall grade to a B, a grade more representative of her effort. Similarly, if a group received a B on the performance but one of the group members contributed very little to the proceedings, an F on his peer evaluation will pull his grade down to a D for the overall representative grade of his effort.

Some would say that when you have students grading on effort, you won't get an accurate assessment of the content mastery. Keep in mind, though, PBA is as much about the process as it is about the final product. Peer evaluations give an evaluation of the students' role in that process. The peer evaluation does not evaluate the final product—that is for you, the teacher, to decide. Much like the group work itself, this peer evaluation must be purposeful and students must be trained on how to evaluate each other as objectively as possible. Otherwise, you get students who might grade down simply because they do not like someone, or students who strike a deal to grade each other favorably even though they did not work very hard on the PBA. What I do for peer evaluations is a running evaluation of how students are contributing to various parts of the PBA. For example, let us consider a performance-based assessment that is a PowerPoint presentation. The process can be broken down into three parts:

1. research
2. creation of the PowerPoint slides
3. preparation for the presentation

The actual content for the assessment will be evaluated by the teacher. The student peer evaluations are looking at the three above processes to determine how well the student lived up to the norms the group established. I typically have students give a letter grade because that is a classification they are familiar with:

- A = excellent
- B = good
- C = average
- D = poor
- F = failure

Students must justify the reason for the evaluation they gave with a sentence or two. I found that when I conducted these peer evaluations as a summative assessment at the end of a PBA, I did not get an accurate view of the students' overall effort. Students were judging based by how well the group did during their performance, and I was not getting a clear picture of the process. When I turned the peer evaluations into a formative evaluation, where every day students evaluated each groupmate and his or her contribution to each part of the process, I received a much clearer perspective on how a student did or did not contribute to the overall progress of the group. At the beginning of the process, I gave students an evaluation that looks like the one in Figure 6.2.

Each day, students had to evaluate their peers with a grade and an explanation. I would model for students what the justification should look like and more importantly, what it should not look like. For instance, there were examples of acceptable grades and their justifications:

- A: She worked hard the entire time, producing four pages of notes that she shared with the group.
- B: He spent most of the class researching causes of photosynthesis, but there were a couple of times I saw him on sites that had nothing to do with our topic.
- C: She was goofing off from time to time, talking with friends not even in our group.
- F: He seemed distracted and was working on his math homework while the rest of us did research.

We also discussed evaluations that were not acceptable, usually because the grade did not match the justification:

- B: She spent most of the time talking to a friend but did manage to do a little research.
- C: He worked really hard, finding lots of good information about photosynthesis and even a great video that he shared with everyone.

What peer evaluations do is make students accountable for their work in a collaborative learning setting. Students are going to be evaluated by the members of their groups, so they must make sure to live up to the group norms. If they do not, there is a chance the group members will evaluate them in an unfavorable way. I find when I have set up the peer reviews well, there is very little I have to do on my part to hold students accountable. The group is already doing this for me. I have very little policing to do because if a student is off task, the group gets him back on task or reminds him of the peer evaluation.

It is also very powerful to track students' peer reviews over the course of the year. Some students are not blessed with self-awareness. Even when group after group gives them low marks because they are difficult to work with, these students tend to blame their groupmates and not take responsibility. These simply are not people capable of seeing the big picture. This is why I show it to them. I keep a running tally of student scores in group work and after each group PBA that I display in the classroom. I do not use the students' names; rather, I assign them a number, but everyone's ratings are there to see and to compare with other peers. It looks something like Figure 6.3.

	Peer:	Peer:	Peer:
Research			
Creation of Product			
Lesson Preparation/ Presentation			

Figure 6.2. Peer evaluation.

1	PBA #1	PBA #2	PBA #3	PBA #4	PBA #5
2	B+	A-	A-	A-	A-
3	A-	B+	B	B	B
4	B-	A-	B	B+	A-
5	A	B	A-	A-	A-
6	A	A-	A-	A	A-
7	B+	B-	C	C	C+
8	A	A	A-	A-	A
9	B+	A-	A	A-	A
10	A	A	A-	A	A
11	B+	A-	A	B+	B+
12	C	B+	A	A-	B-

Figure 6.3. Tally of students' scores.

What I look for and what I hope students begin to see are patterns. For instance, Student #8 seems like a valuable groupmate to have, earning high marks consistently. Student #7 seems to have started the year well but has faded on the past few PBAs. You see a steady progression of improvement in Student #12, although he seems to be falling back into bad habits. Having general conversations about patterns will help students to see the larger picture and be able to self-reflect better on their evaluations. These results are not displayed to humiliate students but to allow them to see where they fall with other students in the classroom. It provides them with context for how their effort stacks up to others.

Successful cooperative learning is one of those things you cannot expect to occur organically. As a teacher, you have to provide a protocol for expectations, train students how to evaluate one another, nurture their development through the process, and give them space to cooperate. If you are able to do this, you will definitely have an effective community of learners.

STUDENT-DIRECTED LEARNING

This book talked about self-directed learning at length in Chapter 1. This is one of the many advantages PBA provides. The use of contracts, calendars, and rubrics allows students to develop the skills of time management, responsibility, and ownership. There is an additional strategy to share for self-directed learning, and that is the act of self-reflection.

Self-reflection is a very important skill for learning. It allows a student to determine what was done well and can be repeated again for success, as well as what did not work and could be changed for the next time. We do not devote enough time for this self-reflection in the educational world. We present information and assess whether students have learned it or not. After we have assessed them, how much time do we typically devote to allowing the students to reflect? Usually none. Reflection is a process, just as working on a PBA is a process. This process involves examining as well as interpreting experience. The goal is for students to gain an understanding from this experience, not just from the content. According to Colorado State University (2014), reflection has the following benefits:

- Reflection transforms experience into genuine learning about individual values and goals and about larger social issues.
- Reflection challenges students to connect service activities to course objectives and to develop higher level thinking and problem-solving skills.
- By fostering a sense of connection to the community and a deeper awareness of community needs, reflection increases the likelihood that students will remain committed to service beyond the term of the course.

■ Reflection works against the perpetuation of stereotypes by raising students' awareness of the social structures surrounding service environments. (para.2)

Just like other activities in the performance-based classroom, reflection must be purposeful. You cannot just tell students to be reflective; this is something they are not used to doing in most cases and will need some guidance on. An easy way to start with self-reflection is to have students complete self-evaluations for their performance-based assessment. This is as simple as giving the students the rubric that has been created for the assessment and having the students evaluate themselves. The individual students and teacher should have a conference to compare the two rubrics. If the teacher and student are close in their evaluation of the assessment, they should discuss what they both saw as being successful and what needed improvement. If the student and teacher have diverging evaluations, the two can share each others' viewpoints and perhaps even compromise on their evaluations. The important thing is for the teacher to remind the student constantly of the descriptors in the rubric and ask the students how their PBAs met those descriptors. If the students cannot provide examples of this, perhaps the students are off in their evaluations. This conference is not about who is wrong or right; it is about making sure both parties are seeing events in the same manner.

There are other activities you can do with students to produce purposeful, quality self-reflection. Here are some suggestions from Carleton College (2012):

■ Oral reflection helps students express their knowledge, feelings, concerns, and frustrations. Discussions may involve the entire class or just small numbers of students. Students can be encouraged to make cognitive links between their academic learning and service experience, through the ORID Model of Reflection (Stanfield, 1997). This model provides a progression of question types designed to move students from reflecting on a concrete experience to analytical and subjective reasoning.

  ▷ Objective: Introduce questions related to the concrete experience (e.g., What did student do, observe, read? Who was involved?).

  ▷ Reflective: Introduce questions that address the affective experience (e.g. How did they feel? What did it remind then of?).

  ▷ Interpretive: Introduce questions that address their cognitive experience (e.g., What did the experience make them think? How did their thinking change?).

  ▷ Decisional: Introduce questions that affect their development (e.g., What will they do differently in the future? How did the experience affect their use of information, skills, understanding?).

■ Journals are tools for critical reflection, but do not ensure critical reflection unless structured to do so. Journals should help students sort through their feelings, think critically, and solve problems. There are many formats of journal reflection; however, the purpose of the journal should be clear and follow a format that the instructor explains and models in class. Faculty should read student journals for both formative and summative purposes.

- Reflective essays are a more formal example of journal entries. They can focus on personal development, academic connections to course content, or ideas and recommendations for future action.
- Directed writings ask students to consider their experiences within the framework of course content. The teacher provides a question from class content and asks students to consider their experience in this context. (para. 1–4)

The main purpose of self-reflection is to show students that performance-based assessments are indeed processes that continue after the performances have been completed. Self-evaluation is part of this process. To skip this step in the process is really missing an opportunity for students to learn and grow from mistakes. It is an extremely valuable skill for a self-directed learner.

SUMMARY

Grant Wiggins (1998) has suggested that an assessment is said to be authentic if:
- it is realistic, replicating the ways in which a person's knowledge and abilities are "tested" in the real world;
- it requires judgment and innovation by requiring the student to use knowledge and skills wisely and effectively to solve unstructured or ill-defined problems;
- it simulates contexts that mirror the workplace or other real-life contexts;
- it assesses the student's ability to efficiently and effectively use a repertoire of knowledge and skills to negotiate a complex task. (pp. 22–24)

By creating performance based-assessments that address real-world problems, promote higher level thinking, engage a community of learners, and create an environment where there is student-directed learning, your classroom will be able to achieve all of these standards, making your classroom an authentic learning environment for students.

Conclusion

Ultimately, teaching itself is a performance-based assessment. You are not given a multiple-choice test to determine whether you are a successful teacher or not. You are expected to perform in the classroom and you are evaluated as a teacher on whether your students are able to perform. Although your school district and state might focus on those end-of-year tests, the final assessment of a teacher is whether his students can perform in the world no matter how they are being measured. A teacher has to ask himself, do I feel comfortable sending students to the next level in the classroom and outside of it? Have I given them skills that will enable them to learn no matter what the method of instruction? That is the final assessment of yourself as a teacher. By reading this book and learning how to provide your students with the opportunities to perform real-world, 21st-century skills, don't you feel more confident that your students will leave your classroom with the tools to succeed?

Keep in mind, performance-based assessment is just as much about the process as the final product. The same goes for your classroom. The process of students going through these performance-based assessments is going to build valuable 21st-century skills that all students should have in order to compete in the global community. The takeaway I hope this book provides is that performance-based assessment is not just a gimmick or another stunt in your bag of teaching tricks; it is the best way possible to teach your students so that they are prepared for the real world. This will change the culture of your classroom and update it to the 21st century and beyond.

References

Arter, J., & McTighe, J. (2001). *Scoring rubrics in the classroom: Using performance criteria for assessing and improving student performance.* Thousand Oaks, CA: Corwin.

Baker, E. L., O'Neill, H. F., Jr., & Linn, R. L. (1993). Policy and validity prospects for performance-based assessments. *American Psychologist, 48,* 1210–1218.

Bloom, B. S. (1956). *Taxonomy of educational objectives: The classification of educational goals. Handbook I: Cognitive domain.* New York, NY: Longman.

Brydon, S. R., & Scott, M. D. (2000). *Between one and many: The art and science of public speaking* (3rd ed.). Mt. View, CA: Mayfield.

Carleton College. (2012). *Types of reflection activities.* Retrieved from http://serc.carleton.edu/econ/service/activity_type.html

Colorado State University. (2014). *Benefits of reflection.* Retrieved from http://writing.colostate.edu/guides/teaching/service_learning/refben.cfm

Dodge, B., & Pickett, N. (2007). *Rubrics for web lessons.* Retrieved from http://webquest.sdsu.edu/rubrics/weblessons.htm

Garlikov, R. (2014). *The Socratic method: Teaching by asking instead of telling.* Retrieved from http://www.garlikov.com/Soc_Meth.html

Glencoe/McGraw-Hill. (2000). *Performance assessment: It's what you do with what you know.* Retrieved from http://www.glencoe.com/sec/teachingtoday/educationupclose.phtml/2

Goodrich, H. (1996). Understanding rubrics. *Educational Leadership, 54*(4), 14–18.

Herman, J. L., Aschbacher, P. R., & Winters, L. (1992). *A practical guide to alternative assessment.* Alexandria, VA: Association for Supervision and Curriculum Development.

Kelly, M. (2014). *Student portfolios: Getting started with student portfolios.* Retrieved from http://712educators.about.com/od/portfolios/a/portfolios.htm

Lopatto, D. (2003). The essential features of undergraduate research. *Council on Undergraduate Research Quarterly, 2*, 139–142.

Mangrum, J. (2010). Sharing practice through Socratic seminars. *Kappan, 91* (7), 40–43.

National Governors Association Center for Best Practices, & Council of Chief State School Officers. (2010a). *Common Core State Standards for English Language Arts.* Washington, DC: Author.

National Governors Association Center for Best Practices, & Council of Chief State School Officers. (2010b). *Common Core State Standards for Mathematics.* Washington, DC: Author.

National Science Foundation. (2003). *The science and engineering workforce realizing America's potential.* Retrieved from http://www.nsf.gov/nsb/documents/2003/nsb0369/nsb0369.pdf

Ohio's New Learning Standards. (2012). *K–8 social studies.* Retrieved from http://education.ohio.gov/Topics/Ohio-s-New-Learning-Standards/Social-Studies

Project Appleseed. (2010). *Performance-based assessment.* Retrieved from http://www.projectappleseed.org/#!assessment/cwvf

Robbins, A. (2006). *The overachievers: the secret lives of driven kids.* New York, NY: Hyperion.

Rule, A. C. (2006). The components of authentic learning. *Journal of Authentic Learning, 3*(1), 1–10. Retrieved from http://www.oswego.edu/academics/colleges_and_departments/education/jal/

Ryan. (2013, July 6). Re: Why is public speaking important? 11 solid reasons why public speaking is important in your life [web log message]. Retrieved from http://publicspeakingpower.com/why-is-public-speaking-important/

Ryan, R. M., & Grolnick, W. S. (1986). Origins and pawns in the classroom: Self-report and projective assessments of individual differences in children's perceptions. *Journal of Personality and Social Psychology, 50*(3), 550–558.

Sanoff, A. P. (2006). A Perception Gap Over Students' Preparation. *The Chronicle of Higher Education.* Retrieved from http://chronicle.com/article/A-Perception-Gap-Over/31426/

Sedita, J. (2012). *The key comprehension routine* (2nd ed.). Rowley, MA: Keys to Literacy.

Stanfield, R. (1997). *The art of focused conversation: 100 ways to access wisdom in the workplace.* Toronto, Canada: The Canadian Institute of Cultural Affairs.

Statistic Brain. (2013). *Fear of public speaking statistics.* Retrieved from http://www. statisticbrain.com/fear-of-public-speaking-statistics/

Stevenson, S. (2001). *Performance-based assessment.* Retrieved from http://people.cs. clemson.edu/~steve/CW/Info/performance.html

Trilling, B., & Fadel, C. (2009). *21st-century skills: Learning for life in our times.* Hoboken, NJ: Jossey-Bass.

Wenglinsky, H. (2000). *How teaching matters: Bringing the classroom back into discussions of teacher quality.* Princeton, NJ: Educational Testing Service.

Wenglinsky, H. (2002). How schools matter: The link between teacher classroom practices and student academic performance. *Educational Policy Analysis Archives, 10,* 12. Retrieved from http://epaa.asu.edu/epaa/v10n12/

Wenglinsky, H. (2003). Using large-scale research to gauge the impact of instructional practices on student reading comprehension: An exploratory study. *Education Policy Analysis Archives, 11,* 19. Retrieved from http://epaa.asu.edu/apaa/v11n19/

Wenglinsky, H. (2004). Facts or critical thinking skills? What NAEP results say. *Educational Leadership, 62*(1), 32–35.

Wiggins, G. (1998). *Educative assessment: Designing assessments to inform and improve student performance.* San Francisco, CA: Jossey-Bass.

APPENDIX A

Reproducibles

LITERATURE CIRCLE QUESTIONS TO PONDER

1. Give a brief overview of what the book is about. Imagine you are writing the back cover of the book for the publisher and you need to convince customers picking it up in the store to read the book. What parts of the story would you share to get them to do that? What parts would you leave out so that you do not ruin the book for them?

2. Pretend you are a book reviewer working for the newspaper. They've asked you to write a review of the book for their readers. What is your opinion of the book and characters? What type of person/reader would enjoy reading this book? Be sure to support your opinions with proof from the story.

3. Which character in the book is the most like you? Tell us who that character is, and why he or she is similar to you. Make sure to give examples from the story. Think about these things:
   - personality,
   - hobbies,
   - opinions, and
   - family.

4. After reading the whole book, tell us if you would want to be a character in this story or not. Make sure you describe at least three events from the story and tell us why those events either would or would not make you want to be part of this story. Think about these things:
   - Were the characters people you would want to be around?
   - Were the events in the story events that you would want to be involved in?
   - Was it a time period that you would like to live in?

5. If you could change one part about this book, what would it be and why? First explain the part in detail. Then describe why you would want to change the part. Finally, show what you would do differently.

6. If you enjoyed the book and don't want to change anything, which part of the book would you like to expand? Maybe you want to know more about a relationship between two characters, or maybe you want to know more about a scene. Make sure you include why you want to know more.

7. If you were to write a sequel to the book, what would it be about? Why would you choose that particular storyline? Would you bring back all of the characters? Why or why not?

8. If you could write this book from another character's point of view, whose would you choose? Why would you choose him or her? How would this change the story and why?

LESSON PLAN TEMPLATE

Name of Lesson: _____

Learning Objectives:

- _____
- _____
- _____

Materials Needed:

- _____
- _____
- _____

What Are You Going to Teach (Break objectives down into parts.)?:

- _____
- _____
- _____

How Will You Assess Students?:

- _____
- _____
- _____

FORMING NORMS

Materials:

- Post-it notes
- chart paper/whiteboard
- pens

Roles:

- scribe
- spokesperson
- moderator

Steps:

1. Each person in the group will receive a dozen or so Post-it notes and a pen. Answer following question: "What do you need in order to work effectively in a group?"
2. Take 5–10 minutes to write down ideas for norms. Make sure you put one norm per Post-it note.
3. Once everyone in the group has finished, go up to the board and cluster similar suggestions together.
4. Select a spokesperson to come to the board and read the ideas.
5. Elect a moderator, who will lead a group discussion based on the ideas shared on the board. It's important to make sure everyone agrees to a norm before adopting it.
6. Select a scribe to write on a piece of paper or a piece of butcher paper the norms that are agreed on.
7. Someone will eventually need to type the norms up and provide copies for everyone.

INTERNET SCAVENGER HUNT

Practice using a variety of search tools by completing the Scavenger Hunt below! Look for each answer by using the website provided after each question.

1. What are the date of birth and birthplace of Edgar Allan Poe?
   Search: http://www.google.com

   _____

   _____

2. In what year did Ireland gain its independence from Britain?
   Search: http://www.yahoo.com

   _____

   _____

3. What movie won the Academy Award for Best Picture in 1976?
   Search: http://www.ipl.org

   _____

   _____

4. What is the tallest building in the world? How tall (in feet) is it?
   Search: http://www.bing.com

   _____

   _____

5. In 1849, people from all over the world traveled to California in search of gold. These people were known as 49ers. Water was scarce during the trip. Some businessmen in California knew this and began selling water to the 49ers. How much were some 49ers willing to spend on a glass of water?
   Search: http://www.pbs.org

   _____

   _____

Now choose your own search engines and answer the following questions:

6. Who is the "father of modern art"?

   _____

   _____

7. What are the definitions of the following math terms: range, median, and mode?

   • _____

   • _____

   • _____

8. Who was the 24th Vice President of the United States?

   _____

   _____

9. How many days in a year on the planet Neptune?

   _____

   _____

10. What are two meanings of the word character?

   • _____

   _____

   • _____

   _____

INTERNET SCAVENGER HUNT ANSWERS

1. What are the date of birth and the birthplace of Edgar Allan Poe?
   Answer: Edgar Allan Poe was born in Boston, Massachusetts, on January 19, 1809.

2. In what year did Ireland gain its independence from Britain?
   Answer: Ireland gained its independence from Britain on December 6, 1921.

3. What movie won the Academy Award for Best Picture in 1976?
   Answer: *Rocky* won Best Picture in 1976.

4. What is the tallest building in the world? How tall (in feet) is it?
   Answer: Standing at 1667 feet, The Taipei 101 office block in Taipei, Taiwan, is the tallest building in the world.

5. In 1849, people from all over the world—known as 49ers—traveled to California in search of gold. Water was scarce during the trip. Some businessmen in California knew this and began selling water to the 49ers. How much were some 49ers willing to spend on a glass of water?
   Answer: Some extremely thirsty 49ers paid up to $100 for a single glass of water!

6. Who is the "father of modern art?
   Answer: Cezanne

7. What is the definition of the following math terms: range, median, and mode?
   Range: a set of data
   Median: the number in the middle of a group of numbers
   Mode: the number that appears the most in a group of numbers

8. Who was the 24th Vice President of the United States?
   Answer: Adlai E. Stevenson

9. How many days in a year on the planet Neptune?
   Answer: 60,190

10. What are two meanings of the word **character**?
    Answer 1: A person in a story or play.
    Answer 2: Having strong morals.

CALENDAR #1

Student Name: _____

Name of Project: _____

Due Date of Project: _____

Day ___	Day ___	Day ___	Day ___	Day ___
Day ___	Day ___	Day ___	Day ___	Day ___
Day ___	Day ___	Day ___	Day ___	Day ___
Day ___	Day ___	Day ___	Day ___	Day ___

CALENDAR #2

Student Name: _____

Name of Project: _____

Due Date of Project: _____

Sun	Mon	Tue	Wed	Thu	Fri	Sat

BLANK RUBRIC

PROJECT CONTRACT #1

Student Name: _____

Project Name: _____

Estimated Time of Project: _____

Overall Goal of Project: _____

_____

_____

_____

_____

Skills Learned:

- _____

- _____

- _____

- _____

- _____

Product of Project: _____

_____

_____

_____

_____

Student Signature: _____

Parent(s) Signature: _____

Teacher Signature: _____

PROJECT CONTRACT #2

Student Name: _____

Learning Experience: _____

Objectives	Resources and Strategies	Date	Evidence	Verification	Evaluation
What are you going to learn? Itemize what you want to be able to DO or KNOW when completed.	How are you going to learn it? What do you have to DO in order meet each of the objectives defined?	When do you plan to complete each task?	How are you going to know that you learned it? What is the specific task that you are to complete to demonstrate learning?	How are you going to prove that you learned it? Who will receive the product of your learning and how will they evaluate it?	Advising faculty member feedback. How well was the task completed? Provide an assessment decision.

Student Signature: _____ Date: _____

Teacher Signature: _____ Date: _____

BLANK RUBRIC WITH LEVELS

Overall			
Excellent			
Good			
Needs Improvement			

CROSS-EXAMINATION DEBATE FORMAT

Time assigned to each section can be decided on by the teacher.

1. Affirmative Opening Argument

2. Team Conference

3. Negative Cross-Examination
   a. One person asking questions
   b. One person answering questions

4. Negative Opening Argument

5. Team Conference

6. Affirmative Cross-Examination
   a. One person asking question
   b. One person answering questions

7. Team Conference

8. Affirmative Closing Argument

9. Negative Closing Argument

TEAM POLICY DEBATE FORMAT

Time assigned to each section can be decided on by the teacher. This format puts the students into opposing teams (affirmative and negative) and has them construct two arguments and rebuttals. It uses the following structure:

1. 1st Affirmative Constructive Argument
2. 1st Negative Constructive Argument
3. Team Conference
4. 2nd Affirmative Constructive Argument
5. 2nd Negative Constructive Argument
6. Team Conference
7. 1st Affirmative Constructive Rebuttal
8. 1st Negative Constructive Rebuttal
9. Team Conference
10. 2nd Affirmative Constructive Rebuttal
11. 2nd Negative Constructive Rebuttal

HIGHER LEVEL KEY WORDS

Knowledge	choose, define, find, how, identify, label, list, locate, name, omit, recall, recognize, select, show, spell, tell, what, when, where, which, who, why
Comprehension	add, compare, describe, distinguish, explain, express, extend, illustrate, outline, paraphrase, relate, rephrase, summarize, translate, understand
Application	answer, apply, build, choose, conduct, construct, demonstrate, develop, experiment with, illustrate, interview, make use of, model, organize, plan, present, produce, respond, solve
Analysis	analyze, assumption, categorize, classify, compare and contrast, conclusion, deduce, discover, dissect, distinguish, edit, examine, explain, function, infer, inspect, motive, reason, test for, validate
Create	build, change, combine, compile, compose, construct, create, design, develop, discuss, estimate, formulate, hypothesize, imagine, integrate, invent, make up, modify, originate, organize, plan, predict, propose, rearrange, revise, suppose, theorize
Evaluation	appraise, assess, award, conclude, criticize, debate, defend, determine, disprove, evaluate, give opinion, interpret, justify, judge, influence, prioritize, prove, recommend, support, verify

HIGHER LEVEL PROMPTS

Knowledge	Where is . . . What did . . . Who was . . . How many . . . Locate in the story . . . Point to the . . .
Comprehension	Tell me in your own words . . . What does it mean . . . Give me an example of . . . Describe what . . . Make a map of . . . What is the main idea of . . .
Application	What would happen if you . . . Would you have done it the same as . . . If you were there, would you . . . How would you solve the problem . . . Find information about . . .
Analysis	What things would you have used . . . What other ways could . . . What things are similar/different . . . What things couldn't have happened in real life . . . What kind of person is . . . What caused the person to act the way he/she did . . .
Create	What would it be like if . . . Design a . . . Pretend you are a . . . What would happen if . . . Use your imagination to draw a picture of . . . Add a new item on your own . . . Tell/write a different ending . . .
Evaluation	Would you recommend this book . . . Select the best and explain why . . . What do you think will happen to . . . Rank the events in order of importance . . . Which character would you most like to meet . . . Did you like the story . . .

Mock Trial
Sample Lesson

A. WOLF VS. LITTLE PIG

A mock trial is a good method of performance-based assessment that can be used in several instances. It can be used to reenact famous real cases, such as a social studies classroom that looks at the Dred Scott decision that fueled the flames of the Civil War, or a Science class where the Scopes Monkey Trial can be used as an argument over evolution. A good way to use mock trials with regard to language arts is to bring a book and its characters to life. Whether used at the high school level to put Tom Robinson from *To Kill a Mockingbird* on trial to analyze racism in the early South, or at the middle grade level to simulate a debate between the characters in the novel *The Outsiders* to look at social differences, mock trials allow students to comprehend, analyze, synthesize, and evaluate information from a novel as they put characters from a book to trial.

In the following example meant for an elementary school classroom, students will take the story of "The Three Little Pigs" and determine whether the Big Bad Wolf is guilty of a crime or not. The skill being taught to students is perspective. We are often told there are two sides to every story, which is exactly what a trial reveals. There is the prosecution's version of the story, which is countered by the defense. This is why using mock trials is a good vehicle for teaching perspective.

TRIAL OF "A. WOLF V. LITTLE PIG"

Read "The Three Little Pigs (several versions can easily be found online) and *The True Story of the Three Little Pigs* by Jon Scieszka and Lane Smith to the class. Once students are all familiar with the stories, they will decide the facts of the case and whether a crime has been perpetrated or not.

Questions to Ponder

1. Which of the stories do you believe and why? Is it possible for both to be truthful?
2. Do you think the Wolf should have gone into the Three Pigs' homes? Why or why not?
3. Do you believe that the Wolf did anything wrong? Explain your response.
4. Did the Wolf commit a crime?
5. Is there evidence of a crime? Of trespassing, damaging property, or murder?
6. Is there enough evidence to bring the Wolf to trial and if so, under what charges?

Various Roles for the Trial

In order for a courtroom to work properly, there is a group of officials who manage the daily business of a court. The students are going to play these roles.

- **Judge:** The judge is the chief executive of a courtroom. Providing justice is his or her most critical duty. The judge to see to it that people are treated fairly according to the law.
- **Prosecuting attorneys:** Prosecuting attorneys represent the victim of the crime. Because they are officers of the state, it is their duty to protect society and individual victims. They also need to be certain that innocent people are not charged with crimes.
- **Defense attorneys:** Defense attorneys represent the citizen accused of a crime, known as the defendant. They are supposed to help the accused person after an arrest, continuing to work with them throughout the trial process. The way that our court system is set up, everyone is entitled to an attorney, even if they cannot afford one. An attorney appointed by the state to a defendant is known as a public defender.
- **Bailiff:** The bailiff is typically a police officer who helps the court function correctly. His or her main tasks are to keep order in the court, supervise the jury, protect the judge, and to swear in witnesses.
- **Court reporter:** The court reporter keeps an accurate record of what happens during the course of a trial. This is done using either a stenotype machine or an audio recorder. Many times, the lawyers or even a jury will ask the court reporter to read back something that has been said in court.
- **Clerk:** The court clerk is an administrator who aids the judge in the running of the court. He or she keeps records, prepares jury lists, and provides the judge with proper files and documents.
- **Witnesses:** Witnesses' jobs are to either strengthen or weaken a side's arguments, depending on which side they have been called for. There are two types of witnesses.
  - ▷ An **expert witness** will testify about an area in which he or she has a specialized skill such as fingerprint analysis, DNA testing, or psychology.
  - ▷ A **character witness**, also called a character or eyewitness, speaks about nonspecific issues, such as a firsthand account of the crime that was committed or an endorsement of someone's character.
- **Defendant:** The defendant is the person accused of having committed a crime. He or she is the person that must defend him or herself.
- **Victim:** The victim is the person who is pursuing the case. Sometimes the victims cannot be present, such as when they have been murdered or when the victim is the state, but they are the entire reason the case exists.
- **Jury:** The jury usually consists of 12 people. They hear the case against the defendant and decide based on what has been presented whether the defen-

dant is indeed guilty of the crime he or she is being accused of. A jury is selected from a pool of possible jurors. Every U.S. citizen at one time or another is called to jury duty. During jury selection, both the prosecuting and defense attorneys ask questions to determine whether the person will make a fair jury member. The jury must reach a unanimous decision, which means all jurors must agree on the verdict. This process is known as deliberation, and a jury can debate for hours until it reaches a mutual agreement. If everyone does not agree, even one jury member, it's known as a hung jury, and the trial is considered a mistrial and must be retried.

THE PROSECUTION

The prosecution is responsible for bringing charges against an accused. The prosecution must begin with its *opening statement*. This is a short statement as to why the accused should be found guilty of the crime he or she is accused of. The defense then follows with its own opening statement saying why the accused is innocent.

Then comes the *presentation of the prosecution's case*, in which evidence is provided through the testimony of witnesses in order to prove the defendant's guilt. The defense lawyer is allowed to cross-examine any witnesses the prosecution presents in order to find fault in its testimony. If at any time the defense asks a witness a question that the prosecution thinks is unfair or inappropriate, the prosecution can *object*, which means the judge will either *sustain* and stop the questioning, or *overrule* and let the questioning continue.

When the prosecution is finished, the defense then presents its case using witnesses, and the prosecution is allowed to *cross-examine*. Once both sides have presented their case, the prosecution once again leads the way, giving its *closing argument* first. The closing argument is the summary of why the defendant should be found guilty.

Finally, it is up to the judge and jury to decide whether the defendant is innocent or not.

STRATEGIES FOR PROSECUTION

1. Establish that A. Wolf is a dangerous individual, which is why his nickname is "Big Bad."
2. Show that wolves have a tendency to act violently because it is in their nature.
3. Prove that the alibi of getting sugar and having a cold is, in fact, a fabrication.

You should use your 2 days of preparation interviewing your witnesses and preparing the questions you are going to ask them. You will want to come up with the best questions possible to make your case. You and the witness should come up with the answers together. This is known as *preparing the witness*. Your witnesses are as follows:

(C) = character witness   (E) = expert witness

Little Pig (C): Little Pig is the victim in this crime allegedly committed by A. Wolf. His two brothers had their houses destroyed, and then were eaten. He will testify how after this, A. Wolf came to his brick house and made threats on his life, attempting to blow his house down as well. When this did not work due to the sturdy construction of the house, the defendant tried to shimmy down the chimney to get Little Pig. In self-defense, Little Pig lit a fire in the fireplace that horribly burned A. Wolf.

Little Boy Blue (C): Little Boy Blue will testify he was out in the meadow blowing his horn when he observed A. Wolf approach the house of sticks built by the second pig. Although

Wolf was too far away for him to hear, Little Boy Blue did witness him huff and puff and blow the house of sticks down. After sifting through the rubble, he saw A. Wolf devour the second pig with no remorse and could swear he heard a squeal moments before A. Wolf ate the pig.

Little Red Riding Hood (C): Little Red Riding Hood will testify that A. Wolf has a history of harassment of woodland creatures because she also had an encounter with him while trying to take goodies to her grandmother's house. He assaulted and impersonated her grandmother, attempting to eat Red in the process. Luckily, Red escaped without harm, but felt that if it were not for the intervention of a local woodsman, A. Wolf would have caused her harm.

Office Buckle (E): Officer Buckle will testify having observed A. Wolf running around wildly outside of the Little Pig's brick house, yelling and hollering and making threats. He also investigated the straw and stick houses, finding what was left of the other two deceased pigs. His investigation led him to believe that the houses were knocked down by an immense force and not by nature. While interviewing the defendant, Officer Buckle got Wolf to admit that he ate the two pigs. There had been times, however, when the confession of A. Wolf changed—originally, he had said the houses' unstable structures had caused them to collapse, and only later mentioned his sneezing may have had an effect.

Builder Bob (E): Builder Bob is an architect who has expertise in building. He will testify that even though the houses of the two little pigs were made of straw and sticks, it is doubtful that a simple sneeze would have knocked them down. He has run tests on similar straw and stick houses, sneezing on them, and only one time out of 10 did the houses actually fall down.

Zoologist Jenkins (E): Zoologist Jenkins is a zoologist who is an expert in wolf behavior, having studied them for years. Knowing the violent nature of wolves and their hunger for pigs especially, he will testify that A. Wolf is a dangerous individual and if not put in jail, will commit similar acts of violence. This is because it is the wolf's nature to be a predator.

According to the law, both sides must be made aware of any witnesses the opposing side is going to call. Because you are permitted to cross-examine each witness, you might want to jot down possible questions you would ask each of these witnesses in order to discredit their testimonies. The witnesses for the defense are as follows:

(C) = character witness   (E) = expert witness

A. Wolf (C): A. Wolf is the defendant in the trial of *A. Wolf v. Little Pig*. He will testify that the whole situation is a misunderstanding and that a cold caused him to sneeze the houses down. As for eating the other two pigs, the collapse of the houses actually killed them and Wolf simply ate them because he didn't want the meat to go to waste. He resisted arrest because the Little Pig lit him on fire and the pain caused him to go out of control.

Grandma Wolf (C): Grandma Wolf will testify to the character of A. Wolf. Knowing him for as long as she has, she does not think he is capable of what he is being accused of. She has never seen him commit acts of violence and knows he would never intentionally kill a pig. She will also testify that he indeed did have a cold because he caught it while visiting her while she was sick.

Old Mother Hubbard (C): Old Mother Hubbard will testify that on the day of the crime in question, A. Wolf came to her house and asked for a cup of sugar to make a cake for his grandma. When she went to her cupboard to see if she had any, she discovered that the cupboard was bare and she wasn't able to lend him any.

Coroner Smith (E): Coroner Smith is a medical examiner who examined the bodies of the two deceased Little Pigs and surmised that one of the pigs was definitely eaten after death and is about 75% sure the other pig was also dead before being devoured by A. Wolf.

Doctor Fraud (E): Doctor Fraud is a doctor who will testify that A. Wolf came to his office to treat a nasty cold that he had caught from his grandma. Because there is no cure for the common cold, he was unable to give the wolf anything to help stop the sneezing. The doctor also treated the severe burns on A. Wolf's bottom area. The burns were very bad and must have caused a lot of pain.

Behaviorist Lupis (E): Behaviorist Lupis specializes in the behavior of wolves. He will give testimony showing that A. Wolf eating the little pigs is quite natural for a wolf. It is part of the circle of life and the long-established food chain.

THE DEFENSE

The defense is responsible for defending the accused against the allegations of the prosecution. After the prosecution gives its *opening statement*, the defense gives one of its own, giving its reason why it believes the charges brought against the accused are false.

The prosecution then presents its evidence, calling witnesses to the stand to back up its charges. The defense has the opportunity to *cross-examine* these witnesses in order to ask questions and discredit its testimony. At any time during the prosecution's questioning, if the defense feels there has been an improper or inappropriate question, it may *object*. The judge will either *overrule* and allow the questioning to continue, or he will *sustain* and prevent the question from being asked.

Next, the defense calls its own witnesses to the stand. These witnesses are to disprove the allegations of the prosecution. The prosecution is allowed to cross-examine as well, to try to discredit the testimony.

Once both sides have presented, each side gives its *closing argument*, the prosecution going first. In the defense's closing argument, it will sum up the weaknesses in the case that the prosecution presented and try to inspire doubt in the jury's mind.

STRATEGIES FOR THE DEFENSE

1. Show that the newspapers are portraying A. Wolf unfairly and that he is not the "Big Bad Wolf" they are saying he is.
2. Offer the possibility that A. Wolf truly was sick and that he blew down the houses by accident.
3. Paint a picture of the surviving Little Pig as not so innocent—he provoked the Wolf into the violent outburst that the police witnessed.

You should use your two days of preparation interviewing your witnesses and preparing the questions you are going to ask them. You will want to come up with the best questions possible to make your case. You and the witnesses should come up with the answers together. This is known as *preparing the witness*. Your witnesses are as follows:

(C) = character witness   (E) = expert witness

A. Wolf (C): A. Wolf is the defendant in the trial of *A. Wolf v. Little Pig*. He will testify that the whole situation is a misunderstanding and that a cold caused him to sneeze the houses down. As for eating the other two pigs, the collapse of the houses actually killed them and Wolf simply ate them because he didn't want the meat to go to waste. He resisted arrest because the Little Pig lit him on fire and the pain caused him to go out of control.

Grandma Wolf (C): Grandma Wolf will testify to the character of A. Wolf. Knowing him for as long as she has, she does not think he is capable of what he is being accused of. She has never seen him commit acts of violence and knows he would never intentionally kill a pig. She will also testify that he indeed did have a cold because he caught it while visiting her while she was sick.

Old Mother Hubbard (C): Old Mother Hubbard will testify that on the day of the crime in question, A. Wolf came to her house and asked for a cup of sugar to make a cake for his grandma. When she went to her cupboard to see if she had any, she discovered that the cupboard was bare and she wasn't able to lend him any.

Coroner Smith (E): Coroner Smith is a medical examiner who examined the bodies of the two deceased Little Pigs and surmised that one of the pigs was definitely eaten after death and is about 75% sure the other pig was also dead before being devoured by A. WOLF.

Doctor Fraud (E): Doctor Fraud is a doctor who will testify that A. Wolf came to his office to treat a nasty cold that he had caught from his grandma. Because there is no cure for the common cold, he was unable to give the wolf anything to help stop the sneezing. The doctor also treated the severe burns on A. Wolf's bottom area. The burns were very bad and must have caused a lot of pain.

Behaviorist Lupis (E): Behaviorist Lupis specializes in the behavior of wolves. He will give testimony showing that A. Wolf eating the little pigs is quite natural for a wolf. It is part of the circle of life and the long-established food chain.

According to the law, both sides must be made aware of any witnesses the opposing side is going to call. Because you are permitted to cross-examine each witness, you might want to jot down possible questions you would ask each of these witnesses in order to discredit their testimonies. The witnesses for the prosecution are as follows:

(C) = character witness   (E) = expert witness

Little Pig (C): Little Pig is the victim in this crime allegedly committed by A. Wolf. His two brothers had their houses destroyed, and then were eaten. He will testify how after this, A. Wolf came to his brick house and made threats on his life, attempting to blow his house down as well. When this did not work due to the sturdy construction of the house, the defendant tried to shimmy down the chimney to get Little Pig. In self-defense, Little Pig lit a fire in the fireplace that horribly burned A. Wolf.

Little Boy Blue (C): Little Boy Blue will testify he was out in the meadow blowing his horn when he observed A. Wolf approach the house of sticks built by the second pig. Although Wolf was too far away for him to hear, Little Boy Blue did witness him huff and puff and blow the house of sticks down. After sifting through the rubble, he saw A. Wolf devour the second pig with no remorse and could have sworn he heard a squeal moments before A. Wolf ate the pig.

Little Red Riding Hood (C): Little Red Riding Hood will testify that A. Wolf has a history of harassment of woodland creatures because she also had an encounter with him while trying to take goodies to her grandmother's house. He assaulted and impersonated her grandmother, attempting to eat Red in the process. Luckily, Red escaped without harm, but felt that if it were not for the intervention of a local woodsman, A. Wolf would have caused her harm.

Officer Buckle (E): Officer Buckle will testify having observed A. Wolf running around wildly outside of the Little Pig's brick house, yelling and hollering and making threats. He also investigated the straw and stick houses, finding what was left of the other two deceased pigs. His investigation led him to believe that the houses were knocked down by an immense force and not by nature. While interviewing the defendant, Officer Buckle got Wolf to admit that he ate the two pigs. There had been times, however, when the confession of A. Wolf changed—originally, he had said the houses' unstable structures had caused them to collapse, and only later mentioned his sneezing may have had an effect.

Builder Bob (E): Builder Bob is an architect who has expertise in building. He will testify that even though the houses of the two little pigs were made of straw and sticks, it is doubtful that a simple sneeze would have knocked them down. He has run tests on similar straw and stick houses, sneezing on them, and only one time out of 10 did the house actually fall down.

Zoologist Jenkins (E): Zoologist Jenkins is a zoologist who is an expert in wolf behavior, having studied them for years. Knowing the violent nature of wolves and their hunger for pigs especially, he will testify that A. Wolf is a dangerous individual and if not put in jail, will commit similar acts of violence. This is because it is the wolf's nature to be a predator.

CHARACTER SHEET: LITTLE PIG

You are the victim in this crime allegedly committed by A. Wolf. Your two brothers had their houses destroyed and were eaten. You will testify how after this, A. Wolf came to your brick house and made threats on your life, attempting to blow your house down as well. When this did not work due to the sturdy construction of the house, he tried to shimmy down the chimney to get you. In self defense, you lit a fire in your fireplace and when A. Wolf reached the bottom, he was badly burned.

You will be interviewed by the prosecuting attorney prior to the trial, and he will prepare you with the questions you'll be asked on the stand. You and the attorneys will come up with an answer to these questions, which you will use during the trial. This process is known as *preparing the witness*. You should also be prepared to answer any questions the defense might ask you in the cross-examination. The defense attorney can ask just about anything, so make sure you stay in character and answer as your character would.

Write the questions your lawyer is going to ask you and the responses you will give.

Question #1 _____

_____

_____

_____

_____

Response #1 _____

_____

_____

_____

_____

Question #2 _____

_____

_____

_____

_____

Response #2 _____

_____

_____

_____

_____

Question #3 _____

_____

_____

_____

_____

Response #3 _____

_____

_____

_____

_____

CHARACTER SHEET: LITTLE BOY BLUE

You are a character witness for the prosecution in this case. You were out in the meadow blowing your horn when you observed A. Wolf approach the house of sticks built by the second pig. Although he was too far away for you to hear him, you did witness him huff and puff and blow the house of sticks down. Afterward, you saw A. Wolf sift through the rubble and devour the second pig with no remorse. You could swear you heard a squeal moments before A. Wolf ate the pig.

You will be interviewed by the prosecuting attorney prior to the trial, and he or she will prepare you with the questions you'll be asked on the stand. You and the attorneys will come up with an answer to these questions together, which you will use during the trial. This process is known as *preparing the witness*. Also be prepared to answer any questions the defense might ask you in the cross-examination. The defense attorney can ask just about anything, so make sure you stay in character and answer as your character would.

Write the questions your lawyer is going to ask you and the responses you will give.

Question #1 _____

_____

_____

_____

_____

Response #1 _____

_____

_____

_____

_____

Question #2 _____

_____

_____

_____

_____

Response #2 _____

_____

_____

_____

_____

Question #3 _____

_____

_____

_____

_____

Response #3 _____

_____

_____

_____

_____

CHARACTER SHEET: LITTLE RED RIDING HOOD

You are a character witness for the prosecution in this case. You will testify that A. Wolf has a history of harassing of woodland creatures. You yourself had an encounter with A. Wolf while trying to take goodies to your grandmother's house. He assaulted your grandmother and then impersonated her, attempting to eat you in the process. Luckily, you escaped without harm, but felt that if it were not for the intervention of a local woodsman, A. Wolf would have caused you harm. This shows a pattern of violence in the case of A. Wolf.

You will be interviewed by the prosecuting attorney prior to the trial, and he or she will prepare you with the questions you'll be asked on the stand. You and the attorneys will come up with an answer to these questions, which you will use during the trial. This process is known as *preparing the witness*. Also be prepared to answer any questions the defense might ask you in the cross-examination. The defense attorney can ask just about anything, so make sure you stay in character and answer as your character would.

Write the questions your lawyer is going to ask you and the responses you will give.

Question #1 _____

_____

_____

_____

_____

Response #1 _____

_____

_____

_____

_____

Question #2 _____

_____

_____

_____

_____

Response #2 _____

_____

_____

_____

_____

Question #3 _____

_____

_____

_____

_____

Response #3 _____

_____

_____

_____

_____

CHARACTER SHEET: OFFICER BUCKLE

You are an expert witness for the prosecution in this case. You were the first officer on the scene, observing A. Wolf running around wildly outside of the Little Pig's brick house, yelling and hollering and making threats. You also observed that A. Wolf had a fire on his rear causing him to act even more violently as he resisted your arrest.

You also were part of a team of officers who investigated the straw and stick houses, finding what was left of the other two deceased pigs. Your investigation led you to believe that the houses were knocked down by an immense force and not by nature. Afterward, you interviewed the defendant and he admitted to you that he ate the two pigs. His reasoning for this, however, was that a cold had caused him to sneeze and knock the houses down, thereby killing the pigs. Because they were already dead, he figured he shouldn't let the meat go to waste, so he ate them. There were times, however, when the confession of A. Wolf changed. For instance, originally he had said the houses' unstable structures had caused them to collapse, and only later mentioned his sneezing.

You will be interviewed by the prosecuting attorney prior to the trial, and he or she will prepare you with the questions that you'll be asked on the stand. You and the attorneys will come up with an answer to these questions, which you will use during the trial. This process is known as *preparing the witness*. Also be prepared to answer any questions the defense might ask you in the cross-examination. The defense attorney can ask just about anything, so make sure you stay in character and answer as your character would.

Write the questions your lawyer is going to ask you and the responses you will give.

Question #1 _____

_____

_____

_____

_____

Response #1 _____

_____

_____

_____

_____

Question #2 _____

_____

_____

_____

_____

Response #2 _____

_____

_____

_____

_____

Question #3 _____

_____

_____

_____

_____

Response #3 _____

_____

_____

_____

_____

CHARACTER SHEET: BUILDER BOB

You are an expert witness for the prosecution in this case. You are an architect who has an expertise in building. You will testify that even though the houses of the two little pigs were made of straw and sticks, you doubt that a simple sneeze would have knocked them down. In your opinion, there would have had to be a deliberate attempt by someone to have blown enough air to collapse the two buildings. You have run tests on similar straw and stick houses, sneezing on them, and only one time out of 10 did the houses actually fall down.

You will be interviewed by the prosecuting attorney prior to the trial, and he or she will prepare you with the questions you'll be asked on the stand. You and the attorneys will come up with an answer to these questions together, which you will use during the trial. This process is known as *preparing the witness*. Also be prepared to answer any questions the defense might ask you in the cross-examination. The defense attorney can ask just about anything, so make sure you stay in character and answer as your character would.

Write the questions your lawyer is going to ask you and the responses you will give.

Question #1 _____

_____

_____

_____

_____

Response #1 _____

_____

_____

_____

_____

Question #2 _____

_____

_____

_____

_____

*Response #2*_____

_____

_____

_____

_____

*Question #3*_____

_____

_____

_____

_____

*Response #3*_____

_____

_____

_____

_____

CHARACTER SHEET: ZOOLOGIST JENKINS

You are an expert witness for the prosecution in this case. You are a zoologist who is an expert in wolf behavior and have studied them for years. You know the nature of wolves and do not believe the innocent story A. Wolf has told. Knowing the violent nature of wolves and their hunger for pigs especially, you will testify that in your opinion, you believe A. Wolf is a dangerous individual and if not put in jail, will commit similar acts of violence. This is because it is the wolf's nature to be a predator.

You will be interviewed by the prosecuting attorney prior to the trial, and he or she will prepare you with the questions that you'll be asked on the stand. You and the attorneys will come up with an answer to these questions together, which you will use during the trial. This process is known as *preparing the witness*. Also be prepared to answer any questions the defense might ask you in the cross-examination. The defense attorney can ask just about anything, so make sure you stay in character and answer as your character would.

Write the questions your lawyer is going to ask you and the responses you will give.

Question #1 _____

_____

_____

_____

_____

Response #1 _____

_____

_____

_____

_____

Question #2 _____

_____

_____

_____

_____

Response #2 _____

_____

_____

_____

_____

Question #3 _____

_____

_____

_____

_____

Response #3 _____

_____

_____

_____

_____

CHARACTER SHEET: A. WOLF

You are the defendant in the trial of *A. Wolf v. Little Pig*. You are accused of the murder of Little Pig's two brothers, the destruction of property of both the straw and stick houses, and resisting arrest when the police came and found you yelling and screaming outside the Little Pig's brick house.

You will testify that the whole situation is a misunderstanding and that a cold caused you to sneeze the houses down. As for eating the other two pigs—they were killed when the houses fell and you simply ate them because you didn't want the meat to go to waste. You resisted arrest because the Little Pig lit you on fire, and the pain caused you to go out of control.

You will be interviewed by the defense attorney prior to the trial, and he or she will prepare you with the questions that you'll be asked on the stand. You and the attorneys will come up with an answer to these questions, which you will use during the trial. This is known as *preparing the witness*. Also be prepared to answer any questions the prosecution might ask you in the cross-examination. The prosecuting attorney can ask just about anything, so make sure you stay in character and answer as your character would.

Write the questions your lawyer is going to ask you and the response you will give them.

Question #1 _____

_____

_____

_____

_____

Response #1 _____

_____

_____

_____

Question #2 _____

_____

_____

_____

_____

Response #2 _____

_____

_____

_____

_____

Question #3 _____

_____

_____

_____

_____

Response #3 _____

_____

_____

_____

_____

CHARACTER SHEET: GRANDMA WOLF

You are going to be a character witness for the defense in this trial. You are going to testify to the character of your grandson, A. Wolf, who claims to have been borrowing a cup of sugar from the pigs to complete a cake for you. Knowing him for as long as you have, you do not think your grandson is capable of what he is being accused of. You have never seen him commit acts of violence, and he would never intentionally kill a pig. Eating a pig once it is deceased is perfectly natural. Plus, you can testify that he indeed did have a cold because he caught it while visiting you while you were sick.

You will be interviewed by the defense attorneys prior to the trial, and he or she will prepare you with the questions you'll be asked on the stand. You and the attorneys will come up with an answer to these questions, which you will use during the trial. This is known as *preparing the witness*. Also be prepared to answer any questions the prosecution might ask you in the cross-examination. The prosecuting attorney can ask just about anything, so make sure you stay in character and answer as your character would.

Write the questions your lawyer is going to ask you and the response you will give them.

Question #1 _____

_____

_____

_____

_____

Response #1 _____

_____

_____

_____

_____

Question #2 _____

_____

_____

_____

_____

Response #2 _____

_____

_____

_____

_____

Question #3 _____

_____

_____

_____

_____

Response #3 _____

_____

_____

_____

_____

CHARACTER SHEET: MOTHER HUBBARD

You are a character witness for the defense in this case. You will testify that on the day of the crime in question, A. Wolf came to your house and asked for a cup of sugar to make a cake for his grandma. When you went to your cupboard to see if you had any, you discovered that your cupboard was bare and you were unable to let him borrow any. This testimony is designed to prove that A. Wolf was indeed going to the Little Pigs houses in order to borrow a cup of sugar.

You will be interviewed by the defense attorneys prior to the trial, and he or she will prepare you with the questions you'll be asked on the stand. You and the attorneys will come up with an answer to these questions, which you will use during the trial. This is known as *preparing the witness*. Also be prepared to answer any questions the prosecution might ask you in the cross-examination. The prosecuting attorney can ask just about anything, so make sure you stay in character and answer as your character would.

Write the questions your lawyer is going to ask you and the response you will give them.

Question #1 _____

_____

_____

_____

_____

Response #1 _____

_____

_____

_____

_____

Question #2 _____

_____

_____

_____

_____

Response #2 _____

_____

_____

_____

_____

Question #3 _____

_____

_____

_____

_____

Response #3 _____

_____

_____

_____

_____

CHARACTER SHEET: DR. FRAUD

You are an expert witness for the defense in this case. You will testify that A. Wolf did come to your office trying to treat a nasty cold that he caught from his grandma. Because there is no cure for the common cold, you were unable to give him anything to help stop the sneezing.

You will also testify to examining A. Wolf after his arrest and treating the severe burns on his bottom area. The burns were very bad and must have caused a lot of pain, which in your opinion, would have caused A. Wolf to fly into a flurry of rage that the police witnessed when arresting him.

You will be interviewed by the defense attorneys prior to the trial, and he or she will prepare you with the questions you'll be asked on the stand. You and the attorneys will come up with an answer to these questions, which you will use during the trial. This is known as *preparing the witness*. Also be prepared to answer any questions the prosecution might ask you in the cross-examination. The prosecuting attorney can ask just about anything, so make sure you stay in character and answer as your character would.

Write the questions your lawyer is going to ask you and the response you will give them.

Question #1 _____

_____

_____

_____

_____

Response #1 _____

_____

_____

_____

_____

Question #2 _____

_____

_____

_____

_____

Response #2 _____

_____

_____

_____

_____

Question #3 _____

_____

_____

_____

_____

Response #3 _____

_____

_____

_____

_____

CHARACTER SHEET: BEHAVIORIST LUPIS

You are an expert witness for the defense in this trial. You are a behaviorist who specializes in the behavior of wolves. You will give testimony showing that A. Wolf eating the Little Pigs is quite natural for a wolf and there is nothing wrong with it. It is part of the circle of life and of a food chain that's been established for hundreds of thousands of years.

You will also tell the court how wolves are not violent creatures; rather, they react to the actions of others. In other words, they will not attack unless provoked. The Little Pig insulting. Wolf's grandma would be cause enough him to try and attack the Little Pig.

You will be interviewed by the defense attorneys prior to the trial, and he or she will prepare you with three or more questions. You and the attorneys will come up with an answer to these questions, which you will use during the trial. This is known as *preparing the witness*. Also be prepared to answer any questions the prosecution might ask you in the cross-examination. The prosecuting attorney can ask just about anything, so make sure you stay in character and answer as your character would.

Write the questions your lawyer is going to ask you and the response you will give them.

Question #1 _____

_____

_____

_____

_____

Response #1 _____

_____

_____

_____

_____

Question #2 _____

_____

_____

_____

Response #2 _____

_____

_____

_____

_____

Question #3 _____

_____

_____

_____

_____

Response #3 _____

_____

_____

_____

_____

CHARACTER SHEET: CORONER SMITH

You are an expert witness for the defense in this case. You examined the bodies of the two deceased little pigs, and with your medical expertise you can surmise that one of the pigs was definitely eaten after death and are about 75% sure the other pig was also dead before being devoured by A. Wolf.

Your testimony is important because it agrees with A. Wolf's confession that he ate the pigs after they were dead. It does, however, conflict with Little Boy Blue's eyewitness account that one of the pigs might have been alive when A. Wolf ate him, making Wolf a cold-blooded killer.

You will be interviewed by the defense attorney prior to the trial, and he or she will prepare you with three or more questions you'll be asked on the stand. You and the attorneys will come up with an answer to these questions, which you will use during the trial. This is known as *preparing the witness.* Also be prepared to answer any questions the prosecution might ask you in the cross-examination. The prosecuting attorney can ask just about anything, so make sure you stay in character and answer as your character would.

Write the questions your lawyer is going to ask you and the response you will give them.

Question #1 _____

_____

_____

_____

_____

Response #1 _____

_____

_____

_____

_____

Question #2 _____

_____

_____

_____

_____

Response #2 _____

_____

_____

_____

_____

Question #3 _____

_____

_____

_____

_____

Response #3 _____

_____

_____

_____

_____

THE JURY

As members of the jury, you will need to select a jury foreman who is in charge of deliberation and reading the final verdict. The jury foreman is also responsible for reading this worksheet to the rest of the jurors.

A jury functions as the center of the justice system. They are the peers of the accused, regular people just like them, not involved in the everyday life of the court system. Jurors must make the tough decision of whether the evidence against the accused is strong enough to convict (find guilty) or to acquit (find innocent). This decision is based on the review of the evidence that has been presented, not on opinion. If the evidence leads the jurors to believe that the accused is guilty, then they should vote as thus. If, however, the evidence is not strong enough to prove guilt, then they must vote not guilty.

Jurors should be unbiased, or have no prior judgment on the case before they enter the courtroom. Juries are selected from a pool of potential jurors who are asked questions by the prosecution and defense attorneys to see whether someone will make a good jury member for their case. The lawyers are allowed to select only a certain amount of jurors. Once 12 people have been selected, these 12 may not discuss the case with anyone else or speak directly to the court during the trial. They are only to listen so as to be able to make a decision based on what they have heard.

After the closing arguments of the lawyers, the jury then deliberates, or reviews the case, behind closed doors away from the lawyers and judge. They are placed in a private conference room and must reach a verdict of either guilty or not guilty. They discuss the case among themselves to try to reach a unanimous decision. If they cannot all agree on the verdict, this is known as a hung jury and the accused can go free.

After their decision has been made, the jurors once again enter the courtroom and the jury foreman reads the verdict to the court. If the jury finds the defendant guilty, they must then return to chambers in order to decide a sentence for the accused. They must determine a punishment that fits the crime within the law.

INSTRUCTIONS FOR JURY

As the jury, your main jobs are to listen to the case presented and, based solely on the evidence, make a decision. **Do not play favorites to your friends or find them guilty or not guilty based on personal feelings.**

During the preparation part of the trial, each jury member is responsible for choosing another fairy tale and rewriting it from another perspective. For example, you might take the story of the tortoise and the hare and write it from the point of view of the hare or describe the perspective of the bears in "The Goldilocks and the Three Bears."

INSTRUCTIONS FOR JUDGE

The judge is the key officer of the court. He or she controls the proceedings of the case, and the principal job is to administer the law. A judge is essentially the boss of the courtroom; however, his or her opinion in the case is unbiased. In other words, a judge does not pick sides.

If the courtroom is becoming noisy or out of hand, the judge may call for *order in the court*. If someone misbehaves in the courtroom or fails to follow a judge's orders, that person may be cited with *contempt of court*.

While hearing a case, the lawyer who is **not** questioning the witness may disagree with a question being asked. This is known as *objecting*. A lawyer objects because he or she believes the question is either unfair or improper. The judge has two options when a lawyer objects: *overrule*, which means allowing the questioning to continue as it had been, or to *sustain*, which means the lawyer cannot continue to ask the question.

Your job in this activity is one of the most important. You control the pace of the court case and must keep things moving along. The case should proceed in the following order upon your directions:

- *Will the prosecution give their opening statement?*
  ▷ The prosecution always goes first. Its opening statement starts the case off and sets the tone for what the prosecution is going to try to prove.

- *Will the defense present their opening statement?*
  ▷ This is the defense's response to the accusations of the defense.

- *Will the prosecution call their first/next witness?*
  ▷ The prosecution will call witnesses to the stand.

- *Would the defense like to cross-examine the witness?*
  ▷ The defense can cross-examine any witness the prosecution uses.

- *The witness is excused.*
  ▷ The judge says this every time the lawyers are finished with a witness.

- *Will the defense call their first/next witness?*
  ▷ The defense will also call witnesses to the stand.

- *Would the prosecution like to cross-examine the witness?*
  ▷ The prosecution can cross-examine any witness the defense uses.

- *The witness is excused.*
  ▷ The judge says this every time the lawyers are finished with a witness.

- *The prosecution will now give their closing argument.*
  - ▷ The prosecution will sum up its case and why the accused should be found guilty.

- *The defense will now present their closing argument.*
  - ▷ The defense will sum up the weaknesses in the prosecution's case and why the accused should be found not guilty.

REFLECTION ON TRIAL

Write a sentence or two on whether you agree with the jury's decision of guilty or not guilty. Be sure to defend your stance with two reasons. Then, write a sentence or two about why someone would take the opposite perspective. Be sure to back up this with two reasons as well.

_____

_____

_____

_____

_____

MOCK TRIAL RUBRIC: PERSPECTIVE

Task: Students must prepare and play the role of a character from "The Three Little Pigs," taking on the perspective of that character.

Student name	Student worked on preparing his/her part, completing the three questions.	Student played the part from the perspective of the character.	Student completed reflection and showed understanding for the other side's perspective.

JURY MEMBER RUBRIC

Task: Students must prepare and play the role of a character from "The Three Little Pigs," taking on the perspective of that character.

Student name	Student completed his or her fairy tale told it from another perspective.	Student listened to the trial attentively and participated as a member of the jury.	Student completed reflection and showed understanding for the other side's perspective.

Additional Performance- Based Assessment Sample Lessons

USE OF HALL OF FAME IN A MATH CLASS—HIGH SCHOOL

Creating a hall of fame is a good way for students to use the higher level thinking skill of evaluation. In the selection process for a hall of fame, one must decide what gets inducted and why. These reasons must convince someone else as well so they must be sound and backed with evidence. Equally as important is what does not get inducted. This requires evaluation and the use of criteria. It also requires a true understanding of the person/item/idea/concept being recommended for induction. One cannot make an argument for its inclusion if one is unaware of its impact. This will allow students to comprehend its importance in the context of the world rather than in the vacuum of its field.

Although this particular project is aimed at high school math students, it could be used at myriad grade levels and subjects areas. Grade school students could create a hall of fame about which manners are most important. Middle school students could have a Renaissance hall of fame for which they induct the contributions from this time period that are most important. High school students could rate which of Shakespeare's characters was the most influential and why.

In this specific math project, students can be very creative with the induction exhibit and "acceptance speech." Students could create a cartoon or animated video that has the X in the quadratic equation giving his speech and thanking all the Y's, equal signs, and square roots for "getting him there." In using a bonus opportunity, students can use mathematical concepts to show how they designed the building that the "ceremony" is being held in.

MATH HALL OF FAME—ASSIGNMENT SHEET

There are all sorts of hall of fames: sports, music, motorcycles, inventions, etc. You have been charged with creating a hall of fame that awards mathematical concepts. You will choose five concepts from mathematics that will be inducted into the hall of fame. Decisions you will have to make.

- What makes it in? What doesn't?
- What is the concept and why is it important?
- What advances has this concept allowed?
- What long-term effects has it led to?
- How would the world of math be without it?

You and a partner will present these decisions to the class for consideration. Once you have these, your group must choose the top two ideas. For one of these, you will create an exhibit that will be displayed in the hall of fame. For the other one you must present a video of its acceptance speech into the hall.

You will be graded on the following three criteria:

- Presentation
- Content
- Display

Bonus Opportunity: Design the building/make a model of where the Hall of Fame will be housed and how mathematics influenced the design and construction.

Steps in the Process

1. Discussion of the project
2. Selection of a partner and the role each will play
3. Brainstorming of possible mathematical concepts
4. Narrowing down or selection of mathematical concepts
5. Research of the concepts
6. Discussion of their long-term effects
7. Creation of the display in the hall of fame
8. Planning and filming of the acceptance speech in the hall of fame
9. Practice for the presentation
10. Presentation including showing the acceptance video

MATHEMATICS HALL OF FAME RUBRIC

Student: _____   Concepts: _____

Overall	Content (Total Pts.: ___/50)	Presentation (Total Pts.: ___/50)	Display (Total Pts.: ___/50)
Excellent (A)	▪ Student chooses five solid ideas to submit to the Hall of Fame (9–10 points). ▪ Makes a clear argument for why each item should be considered for the Hall of Fame (18–20 points). ▪ Shows the long-term effect of all of the ideas and the impact they have had on the world (18–20 points).	▪ Speaker presents clearly consistently throughout, do not read to the audience (9–10 points). ▪ Presentation is organized in a professional manner, making it easy to follow what is being discussed at any given time (9–10 points). ▪ Acceptance speech captures the importance of the concept, providing much evidence and makes the audience understand its inclusion into the hall (9–10).	▪ Display looks professional, like something that would be on display in a museum (6 points). ▪ Display clearly captures the idea form mathematics it is meant to (8 points). ▪ Display is easy for people to view, showing many details about the ideas from the mathematical concept (6 points).
Good (B–C)	▪ Student chooses five ideas to submit to the Hall of Fame, but a couple are not solid choices (7–8 points). ▪ Makes an argument for why most of the items should be considered for the Hall of Fame but not all 10 (14–17 points). ▪ Shows the long-term effect of most of the ideas and the impact they have had on the world, but not all (14–17 points).	▪ Speaker presents clearly most times, reads to audience only occasionally (7–10 points). ▪ Presentation is organized, making it easy to follow what is being discussed, but not as professional as it could be (7–10 points). ▪ Acceptance speech captures the importance of the concept, but could use more evidence to make its case (7–10 points).	▪ Display looks somewhat professional, like a good-quality school project (5 points). ▪ Display captures most of the idea it is meant to, but leaves a few parts out that should be included (6–7 points). ▪ Display can be viewed but some details are difficult to see (5 points).

Overall	Content (Total Pts.: ___/50)	Presentation (Total Pts.: ___/50)	Display (Total Pts.: ___/50)
Needs Improvement (D–F)	■ Student chooses fewer than five ideas to submit to the Hall of Fame (0–6 points). ■ Makes a clumsy argument for why each item should be considered for the Hall of Fame, not really providing substance (0–13 points). ■ Does not show the long-term effect of many of the ideas and the impact they have had on the world (0–13 points).	■ Speakers do not present clearly, often reading to the audience (0–6 points). ■ Presentation is not organized, making it difficult to follow what is being discussed at any given time (0–6 points). ■ Acceptance speech does not capture the importance of the concept and it is not clear to audience why it was included into the Hall of Fame (0–6 points).	■ Display does not look professional, like something an elementary student would make (0–4 points). ■ Display does not capture the idea it is mean to, causing confusion (0–5 points). ■ Display is not easy for people to view, leaving out many important details (0–4 points).

Total: _____ /100

USE OF RESEARCH PAPER IN A SCIENCE CLASS—ELEMENTARY TO MIDDLE SCHOOL

Research papers are a good mix of many skills. One thing to make clear with students is that there is a large difference between a book report and a research paper. A book report does just that: reports information that has already been given, which is lower level thinking. On the other hand, a research paper creates something new. The students take information and add their own thoughts and observations. This reaches the higher level of synthesis. There are easy ways to incorporate analysis and evaluation, both of which are also higher levels of thinking. In order to achieve these high levels, you need to encourage students by asking them higher order questions. In addition to a strong outline to work from, you have to set up a classroom environment that empowers students. They are scientists, historians, mathematicians, or literary scholars. Students need to understand that they are just as capable of creating something as someone working in a lab or a university. Once students feel confident to do this, they will be able to produce performance-based assessments that take the lid off of learning.

Research papers can be used at all grade levels. This zoo project was originally done with third graders but could be used with middle school students. Research papers are also a good way to conduct interdisciplinary lessons. The language arts and social studies teachers could work together to write a research paper involving Westward Expansion and its effect on the United States. The science and math teachers could have students conducting research experiments and writing up their findings with mathematical equations. Whatever you choose, make sure you understand that writing is not meant for language arts only. In order to create strong writers, students should be using this skill across the curriculum.

RESEARCH PAPER—ASSIGNMENT SHEET

We are going to be working on a research paper concerning an animal from the zoo with each student studying a different animal. You will need to invite a mentor to attend the field trip to the zoo so that you can have the time to independently study the animal you are researching. Your end product will be a research paper combining book and Internet research along with your observations of the animal.

Timeline:

1. Arrange to get a zoo mentor to attend the field trip with you.
2. Complete the Initial Interest Research Form and select an animal. Begin to collect Internet and book research.
3. Take the research you have collected and apply it to the research paper outline, answering its questions in complete sentences.
4. Begin to write the rough draft of the research paper. Use the research you collected to write your draft.
5. Go on the field trip to the zoo recording observations of the animal. Complete the Zoo Animal Observations sheet.
6. Write a final draft of the research paper, adding your observations of the animal and conclusions.

INITIAL INTEREST RESEARCH FORM

Choose three animals you would most be interested in learning about and research them on the Internet. From this information, narrow it down to a top choice. You may or may not get this choice so be sure to have a ready backup.

Animals to choose from:

- Gorilla
- Bonobo
- Kangaroo
- Koala
- Orangutans
- Komodo dragon
- Gibbon
- Black bear
- River otter

- Bald Eagle
- Bobcat
- Cougar
- Bison
- Lion
- Rhino
- Elephant
- Manatee
- Chameleon

- Burmese python
- Siamese crocodile
- Giant tortoise
- Leopard
- Black swan
- Prairie dog
- Moose

What do you already know about this animal?

_____

_____

_____

_____

Why would you be interested in learning more about it?

_____

_____

_____

What challenges do you think you might encounter in picking this animal?

_____

_____

_____

_____

RESEARCH PAPER OUTLINE

Introduction

- What animal are you studying?
- Why did you choose to learn about this animal?
- What do you hope to learn?

Life Cycle

- What is this animal's primary food?
- Where does this animal fall on the food chain?
- What is this animal's typical life cycle?
- Are there other animals this animal may have evolved from? What leads you to believe this?
- How does the animal's structure relate directly to its survival?

Habitat

- What habitat does the animal live in?
- What about the animal makes this a good habitat to live in?
- What other animals live in this habitat and how does this animal interact with them?
- Do you think this animal could survive in a different habitat?
- How might changes in the animal's habitat be helpful or harmful? Use specific examples.

Observations

- While at the zoo, what did you notice about this animal?
- Did the zoo do a good job of setting up the proper habitat for the animal?
- What improvements do you think could be made to the habitat to make it better for the animal?
- What other animals are included in the exhibit and how do they fit with your animal?
- Why do you think this animal is a good representative of the habitat the zoo has placed it in?

Conclusion

- How did your research and observations of the animal complement one another?
- What was the most interesting thing you learned about your animal?

ZOO ANIMAL OBSERVATIONS

While at the zoo you will need to make your personal observations of the animal you are studying. This should not just be a reporting of the activities the animal is doing but also your reflections on what's happening. Add as much of your insight and thoughts as possible. Record your observation in detail on another sheet of paper. These are the things to consider:

1. What did you notice about this animal?
2. Did the zoo do a good job of setting up the proper habitat for the animal?
3. What improvements do you think could be made to the habitat to make it better for the animal?
4. What other animals are included in the exhibit and how do they fit with your animal?
5. Why do you think this animal is a good representative of the habitat the zoo has placed them in?

ANIMAL RESEARCH PAPER RUBRIC

Student: _____   Topic: _____

	Content	Organization	The WHY	Grammar
Excellent	- Uses lots of good information to complete Sections 2 and 3. - Observations for Section 4 are insightful and include student reflection. - Shows a thorough understanding of the topic.	- Paper follows a clear, logical order. - Follows the outline completely.	- Answers the WHY of responses, giving a complete explanation. - Uses examples to illustrate points and includes lots of detail.	- Has few or no errors in spelling, grammar, or usage. - Sentences are organized and make sense, one leading into the next.
Good	- Uses information to complete sections 2 and 3 but some more could be used to make clearer. - Observations for section 4 are a play by play that do not include any student reflections. - Shows understanding of major points but limited understanding of details.	- Paper follows a clear, logical order but gets off track sometimes. - Follows most of the outline but some topics not addressed.	- Answers the WHY in a basic manner but does not provide a complete explanation. - Uses examples to illustrate some points but lacking in other places or not enough detail.	- Has many errors in spelling, grammar, or usage. - Sentences are organized but do not flow into one another, causing some to jump around or be choppy.
Needs Improvement	- Does not use much information to complete sections 2 and 3. Leaves more questions than answers. - Observations for section 4 are minimal without much in the description of what was seen or the students reflections on these. - Shows lack of understanding about key points.	- Paper lacks direction or is confusing. - Does not follow the outline leaving a lot of questions unanswered.	- Does not include answering the WHY of responses. - Does not use many examples or lacks detail where it really can be used.	- Errors in spelling, grammar, or usage interfere with the meaning of the paper. - Sentences are not organized and there is no logical flow to the paper.

USE OF DEBATE IN A SOCIAL STUDIES CLASSROOM—MIDDLE SCHOOL

Debate is a natural way for students to experience multiple perspectives on a topic. The class gets to hear various viewpoints on an argument and decide for themselves which to take. Having students argue something they do not necessarily agree with is a good way to get them to see an issue from all sides. If students must get up and argue for something they are diametrically opposed to, it will force them to understand the other viewpoint in order to argue it. Although this might not change a student's opinion, it will hopefully provide some insight. In addition, staging a debate in which the students must play historical roles can be very powerful in helping them to understand what life must have been like during that particular time period. One of the most difficult challenges for a history teacher is getting students to put their own immediate world aside and experience what life would have been like 20, 50, 100, or even 1,000 years ago. The Constitutional Convention debate for this particular PBA allows for all three of these learning opportunities to take place.

Debates can be used in multiple subject areas. Students could debate in science class, covering topics such as whether cloning should be legal or whether global warming is detrimental. In mathematics, students could debate issues of probability in certain scenarios, such as shark attacks or lightning strikes. In language arts students could debate about whether English should be the universal language or whether Hamlet was indeed insane. There's a world of possibilities.

In this particular PBA, students must combine research with common sense in order to come up with their arguments. Students create placards for their character names and address one another by these names during the debate. You can even encourage students to dress up if you like to get them more into character.

THE CONSTITUTIONAL CONVENTION— ASSIGNMENT SHEET

We are going to hold our own Constitutional Convention. Each student will play a delegate that actually attended the original Convention and will be required to debate a point about the formation of our government.

Each student will be assigned a role and a topic to debate, including the side that the student will take. This will be a one-on-one debate. Each side states its points and then the floor is open for anyone to continue the debate.

You might want to do a little background research on the delegate you are portraying:

- What state is he from?
- Why might this factor into the stance he is taking?
- What other experiences might influence the stance he is taking?
- What was going on in the U.S. at the time of the Constitutional Convention?

Be sure to stick to the following guidelines:

- Remember to back up your stance with as many facts and details as possible.
- Do not refer to things past 1787. You are delegates from this time period so make sure you stay in the role.
- Use common sense to argue most points.
- Your argument should at least be one written page.
- Practice it so that it seems like you are speaking it rather than reading it.

RULES OF THE CONVENTION

- Each side will get to present its case.
- Afterward, the Convention delegates can continue to debate whichever side they wish.
- Each delegate can only speak twice on a subject once it is on the floor.
- No passing notes or talking while someone else is presenting.
- Members of the Convention will listen to all sides.
- Your initial speech will be graded, and every good argument made after that can add to the speech grade.
- The debate will include a recess.

PRACTICE DEBATES

In order to model what a one-on-one debate looks like, have the students pair up and partake in mini-debates. This will help get the students familiar with the debate structure without the pressure of being graded.

Example Debate Topics

- Paper is better than plastic when it comes to grocery bags.
- Math is not an important subject.
- College athletes should be paid.
- Schools should have dress codes.
- States should raise the minimum age for getting your driver's license.
- One should watch only an hour of television a day.
- Students should be separated into classes by gender.
- Who would win in a fight, Superman or Iron Man?
- Which came first, the chicken or the egg?
- Barbie dolls are a poor role model for girls.

You can have a few students reenact their debate for the class. After they finish their mini-debates, discuss as a class in general what made for effective arguments and what didn't.

CONSTITUTIONAL CONVENTION DELEGATES AND DEBATES

Delegate	Point of View
John Dickinson	In favor of keeping the Articles of Confederation
James Madison	In favor of getting rid of the Articles of Confederation
Rufus King	In favor of a monarchy
Gouverneur Morris	In favor of a republic
Thomas Fitzsimons	In favor of a strong federal government
Luther Martin	In favor of a loose alliance between separate states
George Mason	In favor of a three-system government with a fair balance of power between all three
Edmund Randolph	In favor of a three-system government with the legislative branch commanding the majority of the power
William Richardson Davie	In favor of a Congress to which members are appointed
Hugh Williamson	In favor of a Congress to which members are democratically elected
Oliver Ellsworth	In favor of one-vote-per-state representation (New Jersey Plan)
Abraham Baldwin	In favor of two houses of Congress, elected with appointment determined by state population (Virginia Plan)
William Leigh Pierce	In favor of one house of Congress
William Few	In favor of two houses of Congress
Caleb Strong	In favor of a unified national currency
Robert Yates	In favor of different currency for each state
Pierce Butler	In favor of slavery
William Livingston	In favor of abolishing slavery
John Rutledge	In favor of counting slaves in the population
John Langdon	In favor of not counting slaves in the population
Nicholas Gilman	In favor of the president being a single person
John Blair	In favor of the presidency being a board of three people
Alexander Hamilton	In favor of the president being democratically elected by the people
James Wilson	In favor of the president being chosen by Congress
James McClurg	In favor of the presidency being a lifetime appointment
George Read	In favor a presidential term limit
Charles Pinckney	In favor of a Bill of Rights
Roger Sherman	Not in favor of a Bill of Rights
George Washington	In favor of a ratified Constitution
Elbridge Gerry	Not in favor of a ratified Constitution

CONVENTION DEBATE RUBRIC

Student: _____

Debate Topic: _____

Overall	Content	Presentation	Additional Arguments
Excellent (A)	■ Includes many details to make clear the point the student is trying to make. ■ Has many examples designed to back up what the student is saying. ■ Research is from the reliable sources backing up the points being made.	■ Speaker presents clearly, does not read to audience. ■ Speaker uses professional body language, using eye contact, hand gestures, tone, and expressions to add to the debate. ■ Speaker is confident in presentation, showing he/she cares about the argument.	
Good (B–C)	■ Includes details to make clear the point the student is trying to make in most cases, but a few where it is unclear due to lack of details. ■ Has some examples to back up points but could use more. ■ Most of the research is from reliable sources but some does not back up the argument.	■ Speaker presents clearly most of the time but every once in a while reads the presentation. ■ Speaker uses professional body language, using eye contact, hand gestures, tone, and expressions to add to the debate but not consistently throughout. ■ Speaker is confident for much of the presentation, showing for the most part that he/she cares about the argument.	
Needs Improvement (D–F)	■ Does not include much detail, making the point the student is trying to make confusing. ■ Does not use or uses very few examples to back up points. ■ Much of the research comes from questionable sources, is incorrect, or is not present in the argument.	■ Speaker reads the entire presentation or does not make himself clearly heard. ■ Speaker's body language actually distracts from his/her debate; hands in pockets, looking down, or other negative gestures. ■ Speaker is not confident, does not seem to care about the argument.	

About the Author

Todd Stanley has been a classroom teacher for the past 17 years in myriad of positions. He spent the first part of his career facilitating various gifted and performance-based programs and teaching gifted students. He recently had the pleasure of helping create a gifted academy for grades 5–8 in Reynoldsburg, Ohio, called the Gateway Gifted Academy, where educators employ STEM, inquiry-based learning, project-based learning, and of course, performance-based learning. He served as the gifted coordinator for Reynoldsburg Schools for 2 years and is currently in the classroom full-time teaching Social Studies to sixth, seventh, and eighth graders.

He has coauthored four books: *Short-Cycle Assessment: Improving Student Achievement through Formative Assessment, Critical Thinking and Formative Assessment: Increasing the Rigor in Your Classroom, Formative Assessments in a Professional Learning Community,* and *The School Leader's Guide to Formative Assessment: Using Data to Improve Student and Teacher Achievement.* His first book with Prufrock Press was *The Project-Based Gifted Classroom: A Handbook for the 21st Century.* He lives in Pickerington, Ohio, with his wife, Nicki, and two daughters, Anna and Abby.